THERE IS NO BOX

THERE IS NO BOX

Rewiring Your Mindset About Learning

Christine H. Janssen, PhD
with Yogini Joglekar, PhD

MANUSCRIPTS
PRESS

COPYRIGHT © 2025 CHRISTINE H. JANSSEN, PHD
All rights reserved.

The manufacturer's authorized representative in the EU for product safety is:
Authorised Rep Compliance Ltd, 71 Lower Baggot Street,
Dublin D02 P593 Ireland
(www.arccompliance.com)

THERE IS NO BOX
Rewiring Your Mindset About Learning

ISBN
979-8-88926-427-9   *Paperback*
979-8-88926-428-6   *Hardcover*
979-8-88926-426-2   *eBook*

For Omi

Illustration by Katrina Janssen

Contents

	INTRODUCTION	9
CHAPTER 1	THE PURPOSE OF LEARNING	17
CHAPTER 2	SET UP TO FAIL	33
CHAPTER 3	CRISIS? WHAT CRISIS?	51
CHAPTER 4	THE BUFFET	81
CHAPTER 5	D) NONE OF THE ABOVE	97
CHAPTER 6	EXPERIENCE IS THE BEST TEACHER	117
CHAPTER 7	IT'S TRANSFORMATIONAL, MY DEAR WATSON	135
CHAPTER 8	READY OR NOT, HERE IT COMES	155
CHAPTER 9	THE IMAGINARY BOX	181
CHAPTER 10	LEARNING REWIRED AT EDSTUTIA	197
CHAPTER 11	UNBOXING	213
	ACKNOWLEDGMENTS	233
	APPENDIX	237

Introduction

―――

A series of videos on YouTube entitled "Did You Know?" really impacted me back in 2010. They bombarded viewers with statistics, paired with intense music, that showed just how fast our lives are changing. The data was beyond thought provoking. I get goosebumps every time I watch them. The "Did You Know 3.0" version from 2010 included the following data points:

> "The top ten in-demand jobs in 2010 did not exist in 2004."

> "We are currently preparing students for jobs that don't yet exist using technologies that haven't been invented in order to solve problems we don't even know are problems yet."

> "The amount of new technical information is doubling every two years. For students starting a four-year technical degree, this means that half of what they learn in the first year of study will be outdated by their third year of study."

Can you imagine that!? And this was fifteen years ago! We are truly living in "exponential times" (2010).

At that time, I was a university professor and would often share these predictions with my young students during their first semester. These statistics not only blew my mind, it almost certainly left an impression on my students. The room was silent after watching the video. Were we preparing students for this? How do you educate someone for a job, company, or industry that doesn't exist? How do we create lifelong learners and lifelong educators who greet their Sisyphean boulder roll with resilience, maybe even enthusiasm and excitement? And therein lies one of the biggest problems with education in our country across the board.

Within the realm of education and learning, my passion and focus zero in on adult learners who need life- and career-relevant skills. What is taught to adult learners, how it is taught, and why it is taught fuel my fire. I don't just think a better way to teach/train adult learners exists; I *know* it does. And that's why I left my nice, stable job in academia to launch my own immersive learning company, which also led to writing this book.

Even though I spent many years in academia and consider myself a lifelong learner, I wasn't always passionate about school and learning. I didn't even go to college right away after high school. I didn't want to do what everyone else was doing, i.e., going to nearby colleges, often with the same friend groups. This resistance to conformity has been a recurring theme my entire life. It took a few years for me to realize that if I was going to have a decent career and enjoy a certain lifestyle, I needed a college degree. That was the understanding and expectation back in the 1980s and 1990s. I eventually returned to school to earn my bachelor's degree in 1993, but something happened along the way. I fell in love with learning—so much so that I continued on to earn two more degrees. Back to school time was my favorite time of year. I absolutely loved the smell in the bookstore. I was so hungry to learn and be a part of campus life.

That said, over time my perspective of and feelings for higher education changed. For decades, I was continuously either a student or an instructor. I noticed that most educators predominantly utilized traditional teaching methods even though technology and societal expectations were moving at warp speed. Even with the introduction and proliferation of online learning, which has many benefits, too often the only thing that changed was the mode of delivery. We still see recorded (one-way) lectures, lengthy reading assignments with grossly overpriced textbooks, and standard assessments with quizzes or multiple-choice tests. Generally speaking, learning has been and continues to be largely passive. Assessments are too often based on memorization versus application. And even in this digital age, some educators prohibit students from using laptops in the classroom.

Institutions are clearly resisting change. As a result, one of the biggest challenges in both higher education and professional development in the workplace is engagement—or lack thereof. Why we find this surprising perplexes me.

I would be remiss if I didn't acknowledge that plenty of educators believe in using these standard/proven protocols, methodologies, and models. These have stood the test of time, so they must work. Right? The origins of traditional teaching methods, which are still found across our universities and organizations today, can be traced back to the mission of higher education, which, according to the American Council on Education's 1949 report, was "to educate students for lives of public service, to advance knowledge through research, and to develop leaders" (Chan 2016). This mission is more than seventy-five years old. A lot has changed since 1949.

After being a college student for over fifteen years and then experiencing the higher education industry from the inside for over twelve years as a professor, I kept asking myself all sorts of "why" questions.

Why are most formal learning environments and experiences so boring and unengaging?

Why do we accept the status quo?

Why do teaching/training methodologies lack innovation and agility?

Why does tech adoption happen at a snail's pace?

Why do students have to pay so much money for formal learning when every bit of information is available at our fingertips on the internet?

Why hasn't the teaching and learning dynamic changed much over the last fifty years? Or over the last hundred years?

Even within the world of corporate training, organizations are often risk averse when it comes to adopting new technology or experimenting with new tools and methodologies. Undoubtedly, this teaching/learning mismatch exists beyond the walls of academia.

Here are some more good questions: Why am I writing this book? Why does my viewpoint matter?

As a learning junkie, I have been grappling with these issues and thinking about the future of learning—particularly with respect to adult learners—whether we're looking at college students at a university or employees in the workplace. The fire in my belly to drive change for learners led me to leave higher education in 2021 to focus on my own EdTech start-up, Edstutia, which I will dive into later in this book. This business has given me a blank slate and the freedom to create learning experiences that tackle the shortcomings of adult learning head-on. Aside from my professional credentials and my personal experiences as an "expert" student and an educator, I am uber passionate about vastly improving the learning experience, especially with emerging technology.

I am also not writing this book in a vacuum. My coauthor, Dr. Yogini Joglekar, is my partner in crime and the chief operating officer at Edstutia. Her professional background spans adult learning in both academia and corporate learning. She is equally passionate about disrupting the status quo of adult learning and professional development, and she brings a different perspective to the table that is more global in nature. We have both earned multiple university degrees and sat in the learner's seat for decades. Subsequently, we have also stood in the front of the room as teachers or trainers for decades. Those experiences and perspectives about learning have greatly impacted our careers and passions.

It's important to know this book isn't just about our opinions and personal stories. It is chock full of supporting data and statistics, as well as interviews from relevant thought leaders and change agents to provide a holistic, fact-based message. Look at it this way: We are taking historical data and future-forward predictions and enveloping those with our personal experiences, as well as other relevant stories and pearls of wisdom, to present an eye-opening message that warrants action.

I'm here to inform you that the learning experience needs a major overhaul. It has become transactional rather than transformational. Learners are bored and disengaged, which leads to suboptimal learning outcomes. Retention rates are low because of the way we are teaching and training. We are tracking the wrong metrics in the wrong ways. Sadly, students and employees alike often find learning obligatory and a means to an end—such as a diploma or certificate or completing a checklist to be eligible for a promotion or even an entry-level job. In many instances, employees see training as a disruption to their daily workload, which then becomes more of a nuisance than a value-added opportunity.

I'm also here to inform you that in order to drive change, we must first change our mindsets. About teaching. About training. About learning. About the purpose of learning. About the needs of learners. About emerging technology. About the world we live in.

We wrote *There Is No Box* for educators, professors, trainers, professional development leaders, human resources professionals, learning leaders of all flavors, and lifelong learners like us who truly want to shape the future of learning with a renewed mindset. It is for people who understand that the status quo of teaching and training has to change *for the sake of the learners.* Yes, change is hard. Altering one's mindset doesn't happen overnight. But we are up against the wall, and it is up to the learning leaders of the world to lead, not follow.

We will take you back to the roots of teaching and training to understand how we got to where we are today. We dive into why we consider the current state of teaching and training a crisis. We look at the greater implications of the absence of progress and ingenuity in education. We dissect innovative teaching methods and their effectiveness and explain why they often miss the mark. We dive into various factors of our modern world that are challenging—and sometimes downright disrupting—the status quo of traditional learning environments and methodologies. We share some examples of people and organizations that are truly driving innovation in education to spark some ideation. We also look at the forces of change and how to embrace them. Along the way, we will introduce you to new ways of thinking about learning that will forever change your mindset about the purpose and possibilities of learning.

Gone are the days of thinking and acting inside a conceptual box. Gone are the days of patting oneself on the back for "thinking outside the box." This book will challenge your personal stance on learning, help you reframe what learning can and should be, and then set you up with resources, tools, and the will to change. We propose alternative methods and mindsets to positively impact learning outcomes. We provide action-oriented suggestions and resources, as well as a web page associated with the book that includes reports, articles, statistics and more to support your own efforts. This webpage will be updated on a regular basis to ensure you have access to the latest data, research, and thought leadership. This also ensures this book does not become obsolete by the time it gets into your hands.

Adult learning is a Sisyphean endeavor. No sooner have we reached the summit—having guided our learners through the peaks and troughs of their education and corporate training journeys—than their learning becomes outdated, as workplace and societal realities move at the speed of light. The boulder rolls down, and like Sisyphus, it seems as if learners need to start all over again. For Sisyphus, being condemned to roll his boulder up the hill for eternity was a punishment. For learners, it's an opportunity.

The purpose of this book isn't just to read and ponder some new information. The purpose of this book is to inspire you to walk the walk and be a change agent. And our ultimate goal is to help you realize that *there is no box*.

CHAPTER 1

The Purpose of Learning

We learn for various reasons and in a multitude of ways, e.g., formal, informal, on the fly out of necessity, personally, and professionally. Sometimes we don't even realize we are learning. But when it comes to deliberate, more formalized education and training, have you ever asked yourself, "Why learn?" Yogini's son threw her for a loop a few years ago when he tossed this question back at her:

> "Why learn?" My teen's two words brought my teaching high crashing down. We were speaking about his dream career and how applying himself in the classroom and extracurricular learning pathways, as well as social settings (i.e., networking and attending events) would help him move closer to his goal. I had just returned home from my own classroom after delivering a well-executed lesson plan. I told him that *my* learners were engaged. Laughter ensued. We even moved around the room,

identifying and acting out communication styles and practicing business networking skills. I tried to explain to my interlocutor that by learning, you can become proficient and excel at something.

Q: Why?

A: You can earn a living and help others through your knowledge.

Q: Why?

(By now, I was catching on to the theme.)

A: This is Survival 101. You live in a society with expectations and roles, where you are giving and receiving.

Q: Why? I am fine on my own, learning and creating on my own terms, for myself. Don't you always talk about the joy of learning?

The question of "Why learn?" stewed inside of Yogini. The naivete and idealism of this exchange with her son aside, learning and adapting to the perspectives of a new generation (you know, the ones that fill the seats in your classrooms and new hire orientations) is probably one of the most challenging, yet rewarding, parts of teaching.

Think about it. We update our phones, our wardrobes, our home decor. However, we are still learning the same way we did when life revolved around agriculture and rural societies as depicted in an *EdTech Digest* article entitled "Why Are We Still Learning the Same Way We Did 400 Years Ago?" by Kavitta Ghai:

> Since 1635, we have learned in the exact same way in the US: an arrow that points from one teacher's mouth to their students' ears and ends there. One teacher that is in charge of relaying any and all information to their students, with the students expected to simply absorb it and magically become intelligent (Ghai 2022).

Why does the teaching and learning experience remain relatively stagnant? Perhaps because we focus more on the "what" than the "why" of learning. As instructors, we dust off our lecture notes to refresh our memory of key concepts. We might rearrange chairs into a circle for better group dynamics or plan a multimedia lesson for greater engagement. But how often do we think about the "why"? Without preparing our learners for the bigger picture—figuring out how what they learn translates into what they will do in their professional and personal lives—the question of "Why learn?" is not often thought about. We just do it.

Let's play the old word association game. When you hear or see the word "learning," what immediately comes to your mind? What *words* do you associate with learning? Books? Classrooms? Tests? Boring? Maybe stress? It would be interesting to know if you came up with positive or emotionally driven words like fun, exciting, rewarding, fulfilling. The answers will also likely be different depending upon if you are pondering this question from a learner or a teacher/trainer perspective. Those in the teaching/training and professional development industries *choose* to be the one guiding learners. However, most learners are required to complete courses, workshops, and so on as a part of their personal and professional growth journey. To learners, learning is often perceived as a necessary evil.

Here's my next question: What is the *purpose* of learning? Is it a means to an end? Is it because of the possibility of earning a degree, obtaining a bigger paycheck, or getting a promotion? Again, I will likely get different answers to this question, and that's okay because the purpose of learning is morphing over time. You see, for hundreds—if not thousands—of years, the goal of learning was for a subject matter expert to disseminate knowledge or information to others, which they in turn could make sense of said information, develop new skills, and apply them in meaningful ways in their personal and professional lives. Does that sound like a fair place to springboard from?

HISTORICALLY SPEAKING

Now, the purpose of formal learning has changed over time depending on who was being taught and for what skill set. For example, some of the first universities in western society were established in Europe as early as the ninth century to largely groom theologians and civic leaders. By the late nineteenth century, the curriculum evolved to include languages and literature, and then by the twentieth century more humanities- and business-related topics were included in the formal curriculum (Britannica 2025). Why the change? Because of a need to educate more people on relevant topics as civilization evolved.

Consider the Industrial Revolution in the mid-1800s. Given the developments in science and technology that transformed societies, the focus of learning transitioned to hard skills to manage people and machines in manufacturing plants—a rather regimented structure (Maylett and Vandehey 2023). As more career options emerged in the twentieth century, more universities and colleges also emerged. Formal higher education became ingrained in our societal fabric as a necessary step in life for upward mobility in most career paths.

Beginning in the 1980s, the purpose of higher education was essentially to prepare young people for professional careers with an emphasis on management skills. And as we entered the age of technology and the digital revolution, new skills yet again were in demand in the workplace. Over time, we have seen a gradual change in the focus and purpose of higher education in direct response to societal, economic, or global demands. Certain skills, jobs, and careers become irrelevant and outdated, while other opportunities materialize that require new skill sets. It's clear to see the evolution of the purpose of learning focused on the "what" (what skills were in demand, what was being taught) and somewhat on the "why" (industry or global events commanded updated skills), but has the learning experience evolved in step with the learner's purpose?

We can keep turning the pages back to ancient Greek philosophers and how they shaped the learning experience. As noted in *Republic* by Plato, the Socratic method aimed to stimulate critical thinking and uncover underlying assumptions (1955). According to Aristotle in his book *Nicomachean Ethics*, the purpose of education is the development of virtuous character (1902). Similarly, in ancient India, education was intertwined with philosophy as explained in "Indian Philosophy as a Means for Understanding Modern Ashram Schools" (Wijesinghe 1987).

Consider that the "ashram" system in India divided life into four stages: the student, the householder, the forest dweller, and the renunciate according to the *Jabala Upanishad*, an ancient Sanskrit text that was published in 300 BC. Hermitage schools were called *gurukuls* (literally, house of the teacher) and served as centers of intellectual and spiritual pursuit, preparing men and women with religious, political, and scientific knowledge as well as life skills with a guru imparting education word of mouth (Encyclopedia Britannica, 2025).

Fascinating, isn't it? We find the religious and political references interesting and very much appreciate the Socratic method for giving learning more meaning, i.e., to think, to analyze, to ask questions for deeper meaning.

In his book *The Path to Purpose*, Stanford professor William Damon defines purpose as "a stable and generalized intention to accomplish something that is at the same time meaningful to the self and consequential for the world beyond self" (2009). Sir Ken Robinson, world renowned advisor and author on education, describes education as the "two great human journeys": an inner journey to explore the self (grappling with "Who am I?" or learning as feeling) and an outer journey to contribute to the world ("How do I connect?" or learning as doing) (NACCCE 1999).

So, if we combine these two concepts from Damon and Robinson, it looks like they are in alignment with the aforementioned ancient philosophers and systems. The purpose of learning is to prepare learners for a life of social and political engagement and personal and professional fulfillment, and also to accomplish something *meaningful*—not just for oneself, but also for humanity and society.

LEARNING LEADER INSIGHTS

This question "What is the purpose of learning today?" stirs inside our heads and is the focus of many discussions in our professional circles. We have a lot of personal experience and opinions to share from recent years, but digging up all this historical information certainly helps to understand how we got to where we are today as well as the baseline for most formal education.

To round out our comprehension, I recently asked several learning leaders at prominent institutions this same question. As expected, the answers were varied but all thought provoking.

Dr. Bryan Alexander
Author of *Academia Next: The Futures of Higher Education*, Senior Scholar at Georgetown University, EdTech Futurist

"Forty or fifty years ago, people went to college in order to learn for themselves. They learned their vocation. They learned their skills. They learned who they were as persons. And I think that desire is still there. But there has always been a second desire, which is to go to college in order to get a better job, to improve your skills, to use the credential of a degree in order to improve your standing in the marketplace. If we've got more and more people with more and more degrees, [people] have more skills. They are able to improve the quality of life for everybody, the economy, and civilization. In addition, we have changes in our economy, changes in our politics, changes in our culture, and those are all reasons why we have these shifts in the purpose of learning."

Dr. Christopher Dede
Senior Research Fellow, Harvard Graduate School of Education

"In our recent book *The 60-Year Curriculum: New Models for Lifelong Learning in the Digital Economy*, my coeditor, John Richards, and I suggest that 'disruptive shifts in higher education and in working lives require a revolution in educational objectives.' The underlying idea is that we're going to live longer. We don't want to outlive our money, so we have to have multiple careers. And those multiple careers involve reskilling and upskilling all the time to keep up with what's going on in the world. Therefore, it's important for us [as learning leaders] to move from a model of formal education to lifelong learning, and to *empower* lifelong learning, rather than simply empowering formal education."

Dr. Michael Crow
President, Arizona State University

"We're in a world in which universities are basically designed to produce workers for the trailing economy. They have not been built to the extent that they should have been built to enhance the ability of humans to actually fulfill their complete learning potential. Let me give you an example: The most mathematically complicated thing in the known universe is the human brain. Because there are eighty to one hundred billion neurons, and there are ten thousand synapses per neuron, there is nothing at that level of complexity. So why do we have that [capacity]? Well, we don't have it so that we can be trained to be wire cutters, right? Is it so we can really master the interface of our hand with a wooden plow being pulled by a mule? No. We have evolved to the point now in our rapidly evolving world where human empowerment is accelerating, and this is what's getting everybody scared. People don't want human empowerment to accelerate."

"The purpose of learning must not be preparation for work as the key objective, but *preparation for adaptation*, which includes the preparation for work but isn't only the preparation for work."

Dr. Michael Baston
President, Cuyahoga Community College

"Today, learning is personal. There was a time when you learned for a specific purpose, to do a specific task, or to be on a specific track. Well, that's not how it works today. Right now, educational institutions are resetting, recognizing that we can't just offer what we *think* people want, or we *think* people should know, or we *think* people should receive. We have to respond to the interests, the concerns, and the ways in which people want to live and work."

PURPOSE, EMPOWERMENT, AND RELEVANCE

Thoughts and opinions on the purpose of learning vary, but some common themes have emerged during our research: having purpose on a personal level, empowering people to become lifelong learners, and adapting the curriculum to remain relevant with respect to industry and societal demands.

Now, here are the real questions: Do we as educators and corporate learning professionals identify with all of these learning purposes? Do we actively create meaningful learning experiences that matter for the individual and their contributions to society? Or do we favor the "sit-and-get" model of education or training as a credentialing factory, instrumental for better performance but of not much purpose beyond that?

In the early twentieth century, John Dewey emphasized learning by doing and a curriculum that connected multiple subjects and encouraged students to explore their environments. At around the same time in Italy, Maria Montessori based learning on self-directed activity, hands-on learning, and collaborative play. Intrinsic motivation becomes the foundation of Stanford psychologist Carol Dweck's growth mindset concept (Dweck and Leggett 1988). According to Dr. Dweck, "When entire companies embrace a growth mindset, their employees report feeling far more empowered and committed; they also receive greater organizational support for collaboration and innovation" (Dweck 2016).

In the 1980s, educator and researcher Malcolm Knowles popularized the concept of andragogy, the practice of teaching adults, and contrasted it with pedagogy, the practice of teaching children (WGU, 2022). Andragogy theory states that adult learners are vastly different from children in terms of their motivation, the relevancy of the education to their lives, and how they apply that education. In practice, adult learning focuses on giving adults an understanding of why they are doing something, lots of hands-on experiences, and less instruction so they can tackle things themselves. Many adult learning theories developed out of Knowles's work in the following decades, all with the specific goal to enhance teaching methods and experiences for adult learners.

Our vision for the future of learning is to integrate cognitive skills with emotional intelligence and experiential skills. This involves going back to pedagogical movements such as those developed by progressive educators at a variety of learning levels. For example, the "head, heart, and hands" learning framework supported by Swiss educator Johann Heinrich Pestalozzi in the early nineteenth century emphasized psychomotor, affective, and cognitive development in equal measure (Brühlmeier 2010). This is in alignment with learning through thinking, feeling, and doing.

All these methodologies and mindsets have one thing in common: They give agency to the learners and empower them to question, connect, and take learning beyond the realm of theory and memorization. They create environments in which learners connect a purpose to what they are learning. "We only think deeply about the things we care about," says USC professor of education, psychology, and neuroscience Helen Immordino-Yang (2007). Immordino-Yang explains that when learners identify the "why" behind learning, they are more likely to succeed in building memories, engaging complex thoughts, or making meaningful decisions. This is supported neurobiologically as well.

Learning is deeply tied to emotions, which are crucial for memory, decision-making, and creativity. Consider this at an organizational level: Custom learning solutions relevant to job roles and engaging in format can create emotional connections, leading to more effective and motivated learning. It's no surprise that colleges and companies are increasingly trying to identify purpose in their talent pools, because students and learners with purpose are proven to be deep learners and better stress managers (Damon 2009).

Purpose and relevance can be two sides of the same coin in professional development. For example, workshops on new talent review systems held a month away from annual review discussion dates will have a greater impact than those held six months prior to the new system launch.

Relevance is also about interpersonal connections between instructors and learners. Immordino-Yang notes that great teaching encompasses social, emotional, and cognitive aspects along with knowledge transfer (2007). "Great teachers engage with the broader personhood of a student more than other teachers do, and tailor their feedback accordingly" (Woo 2019). What a great way to build trust and create a safe learning space, thereby fostering purposeful, relevant, and empowered learning.

SO WHAT? NOW WHAT?

Providing purposeful, empowering, and relevant learning experiences is critical to keeping learners engaged, which is one of the biggest challenges professors and trainers face. According to a 2022 Workplace Intelligence study on upskilling, nearly three-quarters of millennial and Gen Z employees were considering quitting their jobs due to a lack of skills development opportunities (2022). This lingering disconnect between learners and learning leaders can have a far reaching impact on organizations. When people are checked out, it leads to subpar engagement, commitment, and productivity. This isn't good for anyone.

As we've purported, the purpose of learning in contemporary society is to empower learners to gain and share knowledge in meaningful ways, to fulfill both their inner and outer learning journeys. Isn't the real value of learning when you can do something with that knowledge? When you can grasp new and relevant ideas and skills to apply in your life or career? Knowledge that simply stays lodged in your mind only has so much value. It should subsequently be shared, experimented with, and put into action. In other words, consider that the purpose of learning is not lodged in the present, but it is actually to prepare for the future, for reaching one's fullest potential, and being a contributing member of an organization and society.

Keep in mind that our career paths are no longer linear and predictable, and thus require a *deconstruction* of jobs to *reconstruct* them with the future in mind. "With the speed of technological and sociological evolution we're experiencing, the world is becoming multilinear. […] We know most jobs will be different, others disappear, and others will be created—and we want to be ready and develop our associates to thrive in this multi-linear world," according to global head of strategic capability at Mars, Inc., Nuno Gonçalves (Gallagher et al. 2021). This exact vision and mindset will bring purpose back to so many people.

One of the most poignant things educators should be doing is preparing learners for change, to think differently, to be problem solvers, and to be agile. As Arizona State University (ASU) President Michael Crow shared with me, the purpose of learning today must not be just about preparing people just for jobs, but rather about preparing people for adaptation. Universities can no longer put students through a regimented, prescribed experience as if they were being groomed to be a line worker in a factory. Now, a one-size-fits-all blueprint to follow for uncertainty and disruption doesn't exist, but we *can* put more emphasis on preparing learners for the unknown.

Here are a few things we can do to begin empowering our learners:

1. Ask learners what is most important *to them* in their lives and what makes them interested in the topics at hand. Help them connect the dots so they see the relevancy of learning something new.

2. Experiment with both formal and informal learning to keep things fresh. Action-oriented learning is significantly more enjoyable and engaging.

3. Develop content that integrates both solo and social learning. People tend to have a preferred way of learning that plays to their strengths, but tapping into the collective wisdom of a team can present increased purpose and accountability.

4. Alter your curriculum so the learner's objectives aren't solely about a grade or checking a box. Help them develop a renewed mindset about and appreciation for learning that will stick with them long term.

5. Consider realigning your teaching/training practices to create more effective and inspiring learning environments, whether that be in person or online.

6. Push yourself and your learners out of your comfort zones. This is where change accelerates.

CHAPTER 2

Set Up to Fail

___

THE TRADITIONAL LEARNING EXPERIENCE
"We are set up to fail." Gregory Eddie, a new elementary school teacher on the hit ABC sitcom *Abbott Elementary*, makes this realization and is beyond perplexed (Burkins and Sibberson, 2024). The series highlights the many ways in which teachers nurture student success *in spite of*, not because of, existing learning environments and methods. Unfortunately, this sentiment is all too common in most learning institutions and organizations, well beyond the walls of primary schools. If educators feel they are set up to fail, what's the impact on the students? Do they feel the same—that they are set up to fail?

Who or what determines what the learning experience should be? Instructors? Administrators? Organizational leadership? Tradition? My experience leads me to conclude that it's a bit of all the above. Support for formal classroom environments, lecture-based learning, and traditional assessment methods comes predominantly from the desire for educators to control the learning experience. For example, lecture-based learning can deliver vast amounts of information at scale, model working through problems and questions, and give instructors maximum control of the environment, according to a University of Wisconsin-Madison study (McKeachie 2013). The same study indicates the ease of creating and scoring tests, which greatly reduces instructor time and effort, as being the biggest reason traditional assessments remain popular.

It appears that efficiency is the main reason why the traditional learning model has become entrenched in our system. In Daniel Buck's impassioned defense of traditional classrooms on the Thomas B. Fordham Institute website, he writes, "We use factories because they are efficient tools to produce a high volume of product consistently—in this case, basic literacy, numeracy, and historical and scientific knowledge. Castigating schools as learning factories is not the insult that some people think it is" (Buck 2023). *Egads!*

Let's break the traditional learning experience into a few categories: learning environments, teaching methods, and teaching modes. And let's focus specifically on adult learning, which, in our minds, includes college students, employees at an organization, and any formal education beyond high school. While I have included some examples here and there from more elementary environments, they are included to make a point because the example holds true even in adult learning.

LEARNING ENVIRONMENTS
Close your eyes and envision a learning environment. What do you see? (Come on… try it.) A classroom with a wall of windows, or perhaps no windows? Chairs or desks organized

in rows facing the front of the room? Perhaps a whiteboard or a screen on the wall? An instructor in the front of the room—maybe behind a podium? Or do you envision sitting at a desk in your home office or a small table at a local café on your computer, looking at a Zoom screen full of faces and blank squares? Do you see groups of people? What is the general vibe?

For most face-to-face training/teaching, designated physical rooms or spaces are set up to facilitate learning. But are they really set up for optimal learning? They may align with the facilitator's needs—e.g., an overhead projector to display slides, a whiteboard or two to write down key lessons or guide discussions, and chairs aligned to face the one guiding the session. While you may find creative learning surroundings in elementary schools to spark curiosity and understanding in younger students, you're certainly not going to see this in a typical college classroom or professional training center. At most, you might have a sign on the wall that directs people to the nearest restroom.

Again, there are exceptions to the rule, and some educators go out of their way to zhuzh things up and be really creative with storytelling, real-world examples that are relatable, simplified terms and acronyms to remember key lessons, props like sticky notes, game integration, or chair and table rearrangement to facilitate small group discussions, debates, or brainstorms. Major props to these people for going the extra mile. As teachers and trainers, we do the best with what we have. We have more control and choice when it comes to teaching methods and modes than the environments themselves. In *Abbott Elementary*, "Janine Teagues can't paint her classroom to make it the more inviting color she wants because it is not on the Department of Education's 'color palette'" (Burkins and Sibberson, 2024). Sound familiar? Cue the emergency oxygen masks.

Yogini and I can identify with this from personal experience. While teaching MBA courses in India, Germany, and the US, Yogini had to "disrupt" classroom setup and then put it back to the traditional layout of row after row of desks in front of a whiteboard *every single time* she taught a class. For example, in communications or group dynamics courses, she would put their chairs in a circle to facilitate authentic conversations, but this was not the norm. And while I was teaching in higher education, I refused to succumb to the standard classroom experience, relying on expensive textbooks, droning PowerPoint presentations, and multiple-choice tests scored on scantron sheets. In one of my entrepreneurship classes, which was full of seniors in their last semester, I let the students cocreate the course with me, including how they would be assessed.

People have an expectation and understanding that teaching is done in a certain way. Where does this standard learning format originate? Well, we can find examples of learning environments way back in time with philosophers like Socrates or Confucius. While they may have shared and developed knowledge largely through storytelling, the learning environments back then were simply rooms or spaces where people would gather. The only asset in the room was the instructor or expert. The learners sat around and listened. They asked questions and engaged in robust discussion.

As I searched for an answer to this very question. Wow—did I find a wide variety of dates, examples, and claims about who started formal classroom learning. That said, it seems the initial classroom learning environment emerged in the early twentieth century. What emerged as the de facto learning environment can be seen in one-room schoolhouses: a designated physical room or space set up to facilitate learning with the instructor in the front of the room and desks and learners arranged in rows facing the front.

Fast forward to 2025: This learning environment, with the sage on the stage, still prevails. We see this in kindergarten all the way through corporate learning and development. Why is this? Why hasn't the learning environment or learner experience evolved much? I suspect the investment in physical buildings and technology make it easy—or necessary—to continue teaching in certain ways and in prescribed classrooms. Unfortunately, these static environments are doing more harm than good to our learners.

TEACHING METHODS

As most educators know, pedagogy is the practice or approach to teaching and encompasses the theory and practice of learning. When it comes to adult learners, we refer to andragogy, which is the facilitation of learning for adults who prefer more self-directed learning when compared to children. I've learned that one's approach to teaching, or teaching philosophy, can be shaped by many things: an instructor's personality, the demographics of the learners, what is being taught, the size of the class, and so on. So (thankfully) every learner experience isn't a cookie-cutter experience. That said, some prescribed teaching methods seem to be tried and true and, therefore, continue to be utilized. But most of them stifle the learning experience.

Teaching methods include reading assignments, lectures, multimedia presentations, slide presentations, project-based learning, and more modern techniques such as flipped classrooms, whereby learners obtain new information on their own time via readings and video recordings, so that class time can be used for activities and questions. While the concept of flipped classrooms has been well received, the format still utilizes passive and solo learning for knowledge gain, which to me, misses the mark.

We also know some modern teaching methods, such as inquiry-based learning and personalized instruction, tend to yield higher effect sizes compared to traditional lecture-based approaches. John Hattie developed his visible learning story, summarized as follows:

> Visible teaching and learning occurs when learning is the explicit goal, when it is appropriately challenging, when the teacher and student both seek to ascertain whether and to what degree the challenging goal is attained, when there is deliberate practice aimed at attaining mastery of the goal, when there is feedback given and sought, and when there are active, passionate, and engaging people participating in the act of learning (Hattie 2009, 22).

Despite the introduction of new, learner-centric teaching methods that are more engaging and impactful, traditional methods such as lecturing seem to prevail. For example, in-depth research conducted by Donald A. Bligh is summarized in his book entitled *What's the Use of Lectures?* He found that lectures still constitute approximately 70 to 90 percent of instructional time in higher education classrooms (Bligh 2000). He argues that lectures might be good for disseminating information, but not for promoting critical thinking or inspiring change. We've all been victims of lectures, the sage on the stage in the front of a room delivering content to an audience in a largely one-way format. This is not an effective method from the learner perspective, so why do we continue doing this? Because it's efficient and scalable.

One of the main problems with traditional learning is that it is too *transactional*. Education becomes an input-output mechanism: slide in knowledge, slide out a test score. Joseph T. DiPiro, former dean of the School of Pharmacy at Virginia Commonwealth University and an advocate of hands-on, workplace-relevant learning, pointed out in his article entitled "Why Do We Still Lecture?" that the time-honored method of "presenting" factual material to a group of passive learners is still considered good teaching. But his students reflected that the experience for them was on consuming volumes of knowledge and "cramming" facts in their heads just before an exam, with the outcome of modest retention (DiPiro, 2009). Inputs. Outputs. Mission accomplished.

Now, if memorization were the only skill we needed in our post-learning lives, that might work. Yet the information that traditional teaching rates so highly is overrated—especially in a century when learners and workers alike have unlimited access to online knowledge and resources such as artificial intelligence. Skills such as critical thinking, problem-solving, adaptability, and communication, paired with a zest for life-long learning, will better prepare learners for real-life situations—not their rote memorization ability.

Note: DiPiro's study proved that passive lectures provide the lowest knowledge retention rate. Compare this to active learning that involves discussing actively, practicing by doing, or teaching others, and results in much more effective long-term learning and higher levels of post-learning application. By still relying on traditional practices for the sake of efficiency and control, we are doing our learners a huge disservice.

Raise your hand if you're tired of PowerPoint presentations! We all are. So why do instructors continue to use boring slideshows? Slideshows are still omnipresent in business contexts as well such as meetings, events, conferences, and more, so the workplace perpetuates this kind of disconnected knowledge sharing. To be fair, PowerPoint presentations can have value to a certain extent if used in the right way, i.e., to guide a discussion, explain complex concepts, share visuals to understand a process, etc. But more often than not, the communication is one-way and the learning passive. Give me a white-hot needle.

Aside from lectures and presentations, another favorite teaching method is printed reading materials (or textbooks for college students). Not only is this a waste of paper and money, but the information is all too often outdated by the time it goes to print. Given that the internet was introduced to the masses back at the turn of the century, it perplexes me that there are still so many educators who rely on physical textbooks, bound booklets, or other printed materials such as case studies to share knowledge with learners. We have had the ability to access and share *current* information in digital format for over two decades—for free.

TEACHING MODES

In addition to teaching techniques and classroom practices, another consideration for educators is the mode, or delivery method, used. A teaching mode is the means through which learners are taught. Examples include passive learning, active learning, face-to-face learning, blended learning, distance learning, online learning, and hybrid learning. Different tools or resources are used for teaching and learning depending on the teacher/learner dynamic and geographical location, for instance. Tools or techniques used in a face-to-face setting may not be as effective in online learning—like a lecture, for example. On the flipside, computers are necessary for digital learning modes, but they might not be used, or even allowed, in face-to-face environments.

In the 2000s, e-learning was touted as the magic bullet that would address some of traditional learning's problems. American futurist Jay Cross is widely attributed to being responsible for coining the term "e-learning" back in the late 1990s, coinciding with the permeation of the internet (Bean 2022). It quickly transformed learning in the workplace and, to some extent, at formal learning institutions. According to a 2017 *Forbes* article entitled "LMS 101: The Evolution of Corporate Learning," 77 percent of American companies at that point offered online learning solutions to improve employee performance (Faurot 2017). Variations of online or e-learning have continued to surface since then, including hybrid formats that utilize face-to-face gatherings supplemented by online learning.

Clearly, the COVID-19 pandemic marked a watershed moment for the massive adoption of online learning across all levels of education, from K–12 to adult learning in universities and companies. The National Center for Education Statistics reported that 77 percent of public schools and 84 percent of colleges moved to online distance learning during the pandemic (2022). Due to necessity, the pandemic forced both teachers and learners to adapt to online learning in a flash, and we discovered digital learning modes aren't—or don't have to be—a subpar learning experience.

Granted, we all enjoy interacting with people in person, and learning together in person is valuable, but sometimes various constraints don't allow people to get together in the same location at a prescribed place and time. To me, one good thing that came out of the pandemic was that it pushed us forward to use contemporary technology for learning purposes. This, in turn, altered our behaviors with and expectations of online learning.

A 2023 study of college students by McKinsey & Company found that 65 percent of students and 30 percent of instructors now prefer online instruction (Child et al. 2023). The 2023 Time for Class report published by Tyton Partners, experts in the global knowledge sector, pegs these numbers a bit higher at 69 percent of students and 45 percent of instructors (2023). This preference for online instruction is not because it offers a more active or impactful way of learning. Rather, it is the same rationale that made it difficult to dislodge traditional instruction that makes online learning popular: its efficiency, convenience, and ability to deliver learning at scale.

Unfortunately, it turns out the mass adoption and integration of e-learning technology does not necessarily equate to better learning outcomes. Whether in education institutions or companies, new instruction modes are only as good as their deployment. Even with the shift to e-learning, the dominant method of instruction remains direct and content based. This is despite an eLearning Industry best practice report from 2021 that states that e-learning interactivity and application are the factors that make learning stick (Muqeet 2021).

Content-driven e-learning might have new bells and whistles such as videos, podcasts, and animation, all of which learners tend to zoom through at twice the speed to check the box of having completed a training. The assessment that follows such content-based e-learning—usually a quiz to check comprehension with often blatantly obvious correct choices— seals the feeling of transactional learning: complete learning, get recognition or reward. Box checked.

Even though some progress has been made with online learning or using Zoom to deliver live sessions, the transfer of knowledge from the teacher/trainer perspective hasn't evolved that much in decades. And do you want to take a stab at guessing the completion rate of online learning? The company eLearning Industry has aggregated reports from instructional designers and learners and reports that only 5 to 15 percent of learners complete online programs (Bui 2022). *Say what?*

Online learning is not the end-all-be-all solution one might expect. So many things are missing when we learn online: social cues, serendipitous events, focus, the motivation and energy that comes from engaging with physical objects and interacting with other learners in a multisensory way. Joanne Ong and others highlight why students prefer learning in person in her article entitled "Seven Missing Pieces: Why Students Prefer In-Person Over Online Classes" (2020). It is evident that context is just as important as content when it comes to learning—and optimizing outcomes. This is why we take the holistic learning experience into consideration when creating our own courses or content.

The shift to online learning is a move in the right direction given the fact that it utilizes technology and makes learning more accessible, but we can't rest on our laurels as if we have done everything possible in the world of online learning. More on this later.

THE RUBBER BAND EFFECT
The Rubber Band Effect has various interpretations and use cases. From a behavioral perspective, I see it as the ability for people to stretch their ways of thinking, being, and acting—but only so far—and then revert to a familiar or relaxed state. Stretching and expanding in this sense creates tension. It requires strength and commitment to maintain. Most people would prefer to be in a relaxed, familiar state. It's easier. It's comfortable. This is why so many people, organizations, systems, and processes adapt slowly. Let's face it. Change can be hard. Going out of one's comfort zone can feel awkward or vexatious. Interesting factoid: While we might call someone

who doesn't want to change just plain stubborn, the formal term for fear of change is "metathesiophobia."

I came across some fascinating articles on resistance to change, specifically why people don't like change and what percentage of people actually embrace change. For years, I have jokingly said that 99.99 percent of the earth's population doesn't like change, because that's what it seems like. In reality, that number is much lower. According to Dr. Jim Bright's Change Perception Index report, about one in three people prefer to avoid change (2010). And approximately the same percentage of people will give up on those stretch efforts if they don't see immediate results. *This is important.*

Within the context of teaching and training, we have seen some advancements in recent years in *how* learning is delivered, such as utilizing online learning, incorporating the concept of flipped classrooms, the introduction of Zoom for virtual classrooms, new features on learning management systems, project- or skills-based learning, and more. Now, some teachers and trainers are fighting the good fight and stretching themselves beyond expectations to deliver exceptional learning experiences to their audiences. Even with the progress made during the pandemic, so many institutions and educators wanted to revert to the way things were prior to the pandemic. Instead of a rocket charging upward, it seems people could only stretch so far and just wanted to go back to their comfort zones, returning to their original state like a rubber band.

Why do we repeatedly return to the status quo? For several reasons: Swimming upstream is exhausting. Sticking with the status quo is easier and more convenient for educators, especially when they have many learners to serve. Most educators aren't rewarded or incentivized to take risks or break from tradition. Most of the time they are operating on tight budgets and can't afford to invest in the latest tech tools or resources. In some cases, if they can't quickly produce a positive return on investment (ROI) to senior leadership, the efforts are deemed ineffective.

Without stretching ourselves to try new ways of teaching and training, we remain in that place of familiarity and sameness. That would be fine, I guess, if the world wasn't changing so fast around us. For learners and employees to remain skilled and relevant and prepared for a world of change, they need to be educated on topics and skills for their benefit. As such, this requires the disseminators of knowledge to adapt. It might not be easy to adapt, but it is necessary.

During the pandemic, global HR analyst and thought leader Josh Bersin released a report about the Adaptive Learning Organization (ALO) (Bersin 2020). In partnership with NIIT, a leading learning and development consulting firm, the report identified fifteen key practices that contribute to an organization's success, based on learning strategies that are impactful and relevant. Something that stood out to me is that high performing ALOs evolve. They experiment and innovate. They proactively develop and deploy strategies that embrace change rather than fight it or ignore it. Do you want to have a high performing organization with high performing students or employees? Then be better than a rubber band and stretch yourself way beyond a static existence. That's where you, your organization, and your learners will truly evolve.

SO WHAT? NOW WHAT?

The traditional learning experience as outlined above is the most convenient and widely accepted by education institutions and learning organizations alike. It is the path of least resistance. Even though we've seen a proliferation of e-learning and online learning over the last twenty-plus years, most learning materials and resources on the market support traditional learning environments and methods. Therefore, the learning experience hasn't changed all that much. The problem is formalized learning and professional development are sitting at a crossroads of "If it ain't broke, don't fix it" and a tornado of change.

If you noticed, the environments, methods, and modes are largely designed from the educator's perspective. These are acceptable, traditional, convenient ways of *disseminating* information. But what about the perspectives and preferences of the learners? Some might disagree with me, but I equate education and learning to a company providing a product or service to a customer. The company is the educator. The service is learning. And the customer is the learner.

Now, how often have we heard the phrase, "The customer is always right"?

We no longer live in a world where the company pushes a product, but rather, one where the customer is in the driver's seat. Thanks to social media, public product reviews, and smart market research, companies are hyper-focused on listening to their customers and giving them value-add products and services. If they don't, they lose their competitive edge. And customers.

If you look at almost any other industry that is not offering a commodity, a significant amount of resources are put into understanding their customer needs and problems. This way, organizations ensure they are offering a value-add solution, whether it is a product or service. Compared to other advanced nations, the United States spends the most money on market research, to the tune of 53 percent market share according to Statista. Second in line is the UK, which holds a 9 percent market share in the market research industry (Bohne, 2024).

We are clearly a very customer-centric nation. The industries that spend the most on market research are pharmaceuticals, media/entertainment, and consumer goods. Dare I say that if companies in these industries didn't listen to their target audiences and understand their thoughts, values, behaviors, challenges, pain points, etc., their products would not be evolving at the brisk pace they are today. This is critical for survival in an uber-competitive world.

If we, as educators, spent more resources understanding what our customers (learners *and* employees) want and need, adapting our products and services, and delivering value-added solutions, the learning experience would be very different today. In any other industry, leaders who stay mired in solutions of yesteryear and don't listen to their customers would likely be demoted or fired.

Sadly, educators are rewarded for adhering to outdated systems. They are often afraid to take risks and try new things for fear of potential failure. As a result, customers (learners) are left with subpar choices and experiences that don't keep up with personal, societal, and professional demands.

As I began putting the structure together for this book, I found it difficult to find articles or research that show traditional teaching methods are the most effective. Probably because they aren't. On the flip side, I found plenty of articles and research related to the significant impact that more contemporary learning methods and modes have on learners today. Sadly, this is where the train stops. A lot of research or thought or discussions may show the need to revamp the learning experience, but I am hard-pressed to see a collective shift.

Here, in the year 2025, college students and young professionals are digital natives. They are way more resourceful than previous generations and expect to have access to relevant, accurate information in a nanosecond. Any one of us can learn and, dare I say, even become an expert in something through self-directed learning, skills development, and practical application. Technology has evolved as well, providing teachers and learners with new data-driven platforms, computer graphic tools, video production apps, immersive simulations, and ChatGPT.

In a recent interview with Dollie Davis, dean of faculty at Minerva University, she echoed what we are suggesting. "If you're not student centric and trying to learn how they best learn, and trying to read the room and everything in the classroom first, then you're already setting yourself up for a really hard semester. And you're failing them. You are really failing them in terms of a learning journey."

Building off the previous chapter and the fact that the purpose of learning has changed, I think it is critical that learning leaders stop running on autopilot. We need to put ourselves in the shoes of learners who have different priorities, expectations, and needs when it comes to formal learning and professional development. You might agree with me on many of these issues but are perhaps in the wrong organization. You might disagree with me, but keep reading.

I'm going to share all sorts of stories featuring visionaries and leaders who are doing way more than just talking about change. They are revamping their organizations. They are prioritizing innovation and cultivating cultures that support experimentation and taking risks. Find those leaders and organizations. They aren't at risk of becoming obsolete; they are the leaders and drivers of change. Better yet, if you are in a leadership position, leverage your power to break out of time immemorial, and inspire your employees to also be bold change agents.

It's easy to keep doing what we've always done. But what if you stretched your mindset and your beliefs and your behaviors to be better than where you stand today? Sound scary? What's even more scary is remaining complacent and doing nothing. That's where we as learning leaders are setting ourselves up to fail. That leads to big, compounded problems that become increasingly difficult to fix as you'll see in the next chapter.

The late American actress and comedian Joan Rivers is recognized as the creator of this quote: "Any form of complacency is the kiss of death for any professional." I love this adage.

Now, can we talk?

CHAPTER 3

Crisis? What Crisis?

During my twelve years as a professor in higher education, I sat in countless faculty meetings that often went sideways. They were more like griping sessions, and boy, did people love to complain. What was interesting is that no one was really interested in coming up with solutions. We would get mired in never-ending conversations, such as the pros and cons of converting student evaluations from pencil and paper scantron sheets to an online format—and this went on for months, if not years.

Many tenure-track faculty felt they were untouchable and had no interest in doing or learning anything new. They were predominantly focused on their own research and getting published. Sometimes their personal agendas and demands would bring serious disruption (including lawsuits) to their departments. They complained about everything, from dwindling budgets to the price of an annual parking pass on campus.

We spent so much time making and seconding motions to discuss things that we rarely had time for strategic, progressive conversations. We would inevitably run out of time, so the issues on the table were pushed to the next faculty meeting months away. And this would go on semester after semester. I always thought, *The 800-pound gorilla in the room is that the higher education industry is facing major problems, and no one seems to care.* Faculty were just concerned about keeping their jobs and their individual fiefdoms alive. Damn those students and making sure they're learning the proper skills for future-forward careers! This drove me crazy. And I know this exact same story plays out on many campuses around the world.

This fire in my belly grew over the years, and I had to do *something* to drive change for the sake of the students. So I found myself devouring books and articles about the future of education. There are a lot of great books written by thought leaders on the bookshelves out there. Examples include: *Academia Next: The Futures of Higher Education*, by Bryan Alexander; *Reinventing College: Where Higher Education Went Wrong and What Academic Leaders Must Do to Make It Right*, by Jeffrey L. Buller; *College (Un)bound: The Future of Higher Education and What It Means for Students*, by Jeffrey J. Selingo; *Whatever It Is, I'm Against It: Resistance to Change in Higher Education*, by Brian Rosenberg; *The New Global Universities: Reinventing Education in the 21st Century*, by Bryan Penprase and Noah Pickus; and *The Knowledge Gap: The Hidden Cause of America's Broken Education System—and How to Fix It*, by Natalie Wexler.

Some of these authors focus on the positive and what's possible in the future through a fresh lens. Others delve into laundry lists of antiquated systems and experiences that are begging for massive change but perhaps aren't action-oriented enough. Regardless, the themes are similar, and the problems are real. And one thing is clear to me: Our education systems are definitely in crisis and have been for decades. The combination of ever-increasing tuition, ballooning student loan debt, a disconnect between what students are learning and what knowledge and skills are in demand in the workplace, the devaluation of a college degree, and the inability for higher education to evolve have erupted into a crisis, at least in the United States.

Let's also look at the situation in India and Germany for a global perspective.

A similar story to the United States unfolds in India, where the gap between what's taught in colleges and what's needed at work persists. According to University World News, India has more than forty-one million post-secondary students, the second largest after China. However, the publication points out that enrollment numbers have been dwindling since 2018, with the All India Council for Technical Education (AICTE) citing enrollment as low as 49.8 percent in 2017 and 2018 (Mathews 2023).

This downward trend can be explained in multiple ways: growth in online programs and micro-credentials, the perception of a better-quality education by studying abroad, and the lack of job opportunities after graduation. The Mercer | Mettl report on "India's Graduate Skill Index: 2023" finds that only 45 percent of Indian graduates are employable. This number has hovered around the 45 to 50 percent mark for at least a decade (2023). As far back as 2013, the *Economic*

Times reported that 47 percent of Indian graduates were unemployable (Chaturvedi 2013). These are really disturbing statistics, and given the massive population in India, you know the impact is significant on both individual and economic levels.

To address this gap, private investors such as the Birla Group, Manipal Academy, and Amity University have forayed into the education sector. While these for-profit, private institutions are not constrained by accreditation regulations and able to implement agile innovation and workforce readiness practices, a UC Berkeley Center for Studies in Higher Education research project points out: "[Indian for-profit institutions] really have to struggle hard to balance academic and corporate interests [ultimately meeting neither satisfactorily]" (Gupta 2022).

In contrast, Germany has a long history of established and highly structured school systems. One of the more popular options for young people is the university or Gymnasium track, which has been around *since the sixteenth century*. Since the turn of the twentieth century, students entering secondary education have had a choice amongst four tracks to pursue beyond the equivalent of high school: (1) a university track (Gymnasium); (2) a lighter academic track (Realschule); (3) a technical track (Berufsschule); and (4) a vocational track (Hauptschule).

Having such specialized, work relevant education paired with apprenticeships has been a winning combination for preparing students for specific career paths. The Hauptschule has had as many as 1.22 million students pursuing trade-related apprenticeships as of 2022, which is pretty impressive.

However, Germany is not immune to all the external factors that the rest of the world is facing, such as disruptions with technology, economics, and the impact of immigration on the social fabric of the country. Some are concerned these factors are negatively impacting the quality of education.

On the flip side, international students are making up for dwindling German student numbers in universities and becoming a promising resource to address a looming skills shortage. In November 2023, the Federal Ministry of Education and Research (BMBF) "launched its Skilled Labour Initiative, aimed at recruiting students and graduates and qualifying them as future specialists for the German labour market" (Gardner 2025). This is another great example showing the vastness of the skills gap issue and the fact that higher education isn't prepared to handle the complexities of shifting workplace demands.

Indeed, the German labor market finds itself in a crisis. A record number of employees in Germany—45 percent—were actively seeking a new job or open to new opportunities elsewhere, according to a 2024 Gallup survey. This number has shot up significantly from 27 percent in 2019. The same survey finds that "nearly a fifth of Germany's workforce is actively disengaged" (Nink 2024). In addition to Germany's struggling economy as well as operational and growth challenges, the lack of people-centric cultures in companies is exacerbating the skills crisis with disengaged, one-foot-out-the-door employees.

Still not convinced we are facing a global crisis? UNESCO has published multiple reports over the last several years highlighting where the shortcomings are, despite the fact that lifelong learning is one of the United Nations' Sustainability Development Goals. Around the world, issues around accessibility, low participation, and the digital divide remain, and these things gravely impact adult learners and upward mobility. When you throw in the fast pace of technological advancements and its impact on industry and society, there is a lot of pressure and stress trying to keep up with upskilling and reskilling adult workers.

UNESCO's Institute for Lifelong Learning regularly publishes "The Global Report on Adult Learning and Education" (GRALE), which aggregates survey data, analyses on policies, and case studies to provide a holistic picture of adult learning around the world. Their sixth report since 2009 will be published in 2026 and will zero in on how to manage all the fast-paced changes in our world.

> By focusing on the key drivers of change—such as digitalization, economic crises, environmental sustainability, conflict, and health crises—this report will provide a comprehensive understanding of how adult learning and education acts as a catalyst for empowerment, adaptability and positive social transformation. It will consider the agility and flexibility of adult education systems in responding to the urgent challenges of the modern world and ensuring that learners are prepared for both ongoing and future disruptions (UNESCO 2024).

Adult learning and lifelong learning are top issues for many countries. The challenges are omnipresent.

While we have been largely focused on the shortcomings of higher education within the United States, these issues have vast implications for the American workplace as well as globally. The skills gap, funding issues, lag in adopting and adapting, the need for more systemic change, how to empower learners—these are the common threads found around the world. And indeed, it is deemed a global crisis based on many standalone crises that fuel the situation.

CRISIS #1: THE COST OF A COLLEGE DEGREE
Back in 2012, I was the mother of a two-year-old. I remember watching a news segment on *NY1* one morning while getting ready for work. The topic was, "At what point should you start saving for your child's college education?" The answer was: while he or she is in utero. And then they predicted how much a college education would cost eighteen years from then (so in 2030), and the number was close to $400,000 for a four-year college degree. So… we live in a world where higher education is such a huge expense that you should store your nuts before you even birth a child. We have become so numb to these facts and just accept this is a necessary investment if you want to set your child up for a successful life. Does anyone else think this is insane?

Granted, inflation exists, and students have higher expectations of a college experience. But the cost to get a diploma is out of control—and in many cases, out of reach for a lot of students. We've all heard the news bytes over the years, but let me remind you that the cost to get an undergraduate degree increased 169 percent between 1980 and 2020, according to research by the Georgetown University Center on Education and the Workforce (McGurran 2023). This rate of increase far surpasses the rate of increase of household income, making it vastly more difficult for students and their families to afford such an investment. This exorbitant expense has continued to divide students into two buckets: the "haves" and the "have nots." Wait—let's add a third bucket: students who get buried in student loan debt to be one of the "haves." That was the category I ended up in.

I wasn't surprised, then, when I came across the National College Attainment Network's (NCAN) report detailing how cost was the largest barrier to higher education. NCAN found that "only one-third (33 percent) of public bachelor's-granting institutions were affordable," and "fewer than half (49 percent) of community colleges were affordable." The report states: "The affordability of public bachelor's-granting institutions is especially critical for low- and moderate-income students because bachelor's degrees are associated with higher earnings, lower unemployment rates, and greater economic security for families" (Woodhouse 2024). Low- and moderate-income students face a double whammy: When the door to higher ed closes, the door to job and economic opportunities also closes.

What is an interesting phenomenon is that people are willing to invest $50,000 to $200,000 or more for a college education to get a job that pays them a fraction of that. Some will argue that a college degree results in greater income over time (and there are plenty of data points to support this), but one's upward mobility often doesn't have anything to do with a diploma. It has to do with skills—most of which are learned on the job or in bootcamps or other self-directed learning.

CRISIS #2: STUDENT LOAN DEBT

Student loan history shows the first federal student loans became available back in the late 1950s. In 1965, the United States government began guaranteeing student loans offered through banks and other lending institutions (New America n.d.). While being able to access low-interest loans seems like a great option for students, this enabled institutions to continue to raise overall expenses to students, figuring they could supplement the expense with said loans. And without many other options available to us, we went along for the ride—to the tune of over $1.7 trillion (as of January 2025) (Hanson 2025).

I earned three college degrees between the early 1990s and 2010, two of which were at institutions in New York City. The only way I could attend college was with the assistance of student loans. I took out as much money as possible every semester to pay tuition and keep my head above water. Upon completing my PhD in 2010, I found myself buried in about $150,000 of student loans. (How I dug myself out of that is another story.)

Student loans are quite easy to get, but no one *really* tells you how difficult it is to pay them off. In many cases, people are still paying off student loans in their retirement. And if you follow the thirty-year repayment plan that is laid out for you—and admittedly, the most manageable—you end up paying *twice* as much for that college degree, thanks to interest. Stew on that for a bit.

We are all aware of this crisis but don't do much about it. Sure, some loan forgiveness plans are in the works, but this is a reactive strategy and doesn't address the root of the problem: the high cost of college. To get rid of this student loan problem, we need to make higher education affordable enough that people don't need to rely on big loans. Full disclosure: I do not think *free* education is the solution because the quality of that education would go south. Not the answer. I also don't think it's the responsibility of the United States government or the Department of Education to fix higher education. That change must come from within the animal. And that's where we get stuck.

In such an advanced society as in the United States, formal education and learning shouldn't be so difficult or costly to get. Like any other business, what needs to be addressed at the most fundamental level is value. Is the value of a college degree equal or greater than the cost? And this must be viewed from the perspective of the customer. If higher education isn't able to offer true value to students, they will continue to ponder other, more affordable, value-add options versus going to college.

Dr. Brian Rosenberg, visiting professor at the Graduate School of Education at Harvard University, told me, "The bachelor's degree is still sort of the entry ticket to an entirely different world of employment." He still believes a college education is a worthwhile investment, especially if one doesn't have to go into debt to fund it. But on the flipside, he admits that higher education has been in crisis mode for many, many years. "I think this is a uniquely challenging moment for higher education. And for me, the clear indicators are economics. It has just become too expensive, and people are making the decision not to go to college."

Visionaries driving change in higher education like Matt Alex, founder of Beyond Academics, clearly see the crisis and get fired up like I do. He compares education institutions to corporate businesses and understands that if your business model isn't working, you need to fix it. If your institution is losing money and customers (or students) semester after semester, you need to make some changes or you're going to be out of business. This is already playing out across the country. As noted in The Hechinger Report, another college shutters its doors practically on a weekly basis (Villeneuve and Sanchez 2024).

Alex also fervently reiterates that higher education, as a service provider, needs to offer real value to students. "Higher ed is not sophisticated in a business sense to understand that their model is broken and they have to think differently. They don't actually understand what their value is for their market. They haven't realized their brand value in the market, and the value the students get for their education, and in turn, the value that they bring to an employer. To me, that's so messed up."

If we fix the real problem, there will no longer be a student loan debt problem.

CRISIS #3: THE SKILLS GAP

The lingering skills gap in the United States just never seems to go away or get the attention it desperately deserves. Employers are looking for specific skills, and too many college graduates don't have them, so the employer ends up spending time and money training them. Why doesn't higher ed listen to industry more to better understand the skills *they* are looking for? This disconnect between higher education and employers is vast and real. And it exists because most higher education institutions refuse to adapt to teaching new subjects in new ways using new technologies.

I previously mentioned the videos on YouTube called "Did You Know?" Several iterations and updates of these videos have been created over the years, but the message and statistics are still mind blowing. The underlying message of these videos is: pay attention to what is happening around you, and understand where you and the world will be in the near future. It is a firehose of statistics that show how fast our world is changing, the impact of globalization, how technology is disrupting every aspect of our lives, etc. It's equally uncomfortable and exciting. The 2025 version (https://www.youtube.com/watch?v=FTRJlmN6jeU) listed the following "Top In-demand Jobs Today That Barely Existed 10 Years Ago":

>   Driverless car engineer
>   ChatGPT developer
>   Prompt engineer
>   Drone pilot
>   TikTok marketeer
>   Crypto advisor
>   Zoom manager
>   Data scientist
>   AI architect
>   eSport athlete
>   Cloud architect
>   Blockchain analyst

These thought-provoking predictions resonated with me while I was a professor, and I wanted to make sure my students would be prepared for a world of ambiguity. As such, I adopted what I taught and how I taught. And I think this is necessary across the board for educators, regardless of what subjects you are teaching. Because in many cases we are educating students for jobs that don't yet exist, and they will be solving problems that are unknown to us today.

Plenty of research supports my position on the skills gap:

- A recent National Association of Colleges and Employers (NACE) "Job Outlook" survey highlights disparities between skills in demand and graduate's majors. For example, only 17 percent of employers seek liberal arts graduates, while 74 percent prefer STEM majors (2023).

- Global organizational consulting firm Korn Ferry conducted a study to understand the global skills gap in leading industries. Their report predicts changes to the global talent pool and employment market between 2020 and 2030. The bottom line: "Acute global talent shortages are clearly a looming threat and they're driven by a shortage of skills rather than a shortage of people" (2018, 42).

- The 2025 "Future of Jobs Report" conducted by the World Economic Forum identifies a widening skills gap on a global scale. As a matter of fact, it is estimated that 59 percent of the world's workforce needs to be reskilled by 2030. "Skill gaps in the labour market are the primary barrier to business transformation […] cited by 63 percent of surveyed employers" (2025, 49).

- As noted in a recent *Forbes* article entitled "Mind The (Skills) Gap," McKinsey's James Rappaport states that "as many as 375 million workers globally might have to change occupations soon to meet company needs" (Forbes 2024).

This cute little gap is on the verge of becoming a deep chasm. How are you preparing your students and employees for this? Where do they need to be in a few years? And most importantly, how are you going to get them there? When you look at the transition from student to employee, it appears that the onus to get and keep people properly skilled will more often than not be on employers, because most academic institutions are not changing fast enough.

CRISIS #4: LOW ENROLLMENT
With the number of college-attending students declining significantly through the 2020s, there is no doubt about it: Higher education is grappling with an enrollment cliff. The National Center for Education Statistics reports that undergraduate enrollment numbers have been contracting at a steady rate for over a decade, down about 8.5 percent from 2010 (2023). A *College Transitions* article points to a variety of reasons for enrollment issues, such as birth rate decline, decreased international enrollment, the aftermath of COVID-19, financial aid issues, and doubts young people have regarding the value of a college education (2024). But there's more to the puzzle.

The implications of declining enrollment are realized with more and more colleges shuttering their doors. Over three hundred colleges and universities have closed in the United

States since 2008, and historical data indicates this trend will continue in full force. "At the end of 2024, the Federal Reserve Bank of Philadelphia developed a model to predict college closures, estimating that up to eighty colleges could close next year [2025] due to financial distress following a worst-case-scenario drop in enrollment" (Castillo and Welding 2025).

In response, higher education has become a breeding ground for mergers and acquisitions (Selingo 2025). We are seeing small liberal arts colleges merging to form more stable alliances and networks. We see some larger universities scooping up smaller colleges at bargain-basement prices. Sadly, most of these transactions are more like Band-Aid fixes with short-term outlooks versus strategic endeavors that address the nucleus of the problem.

A 2023 EDGE survey of high school-aged students supported by the Bill and Melinda Gates Foundation points to a diminishing interest in college. Their College Interest Index took into consideration three things: (1) intent to attend college, (2) when they planned to attend college, and (3) perceived value of two- and four-year institutions. Twenty-six percent of high school respondents and 56 percent of non-enrolled respondents (i.e., eighteen- to thirty-year-olds who did not complete high school or never enrolled in a two-year or four-year college program) indicated their interest in attending college as being low (on a scale of low-moderate-high) (2024). The next section dives into their reasoning.

Matt Alex of Beyond Academics, a higher education consulting firm, is very tuned in to this issue and sees a different story unfolding. "The enrollment cliff is an element of a segment of the population that higher ed has decided is who they should educate, and that group is dwindling. But there is a whole market that isn't educated that needs to be educated, and you need to create an offering for them." Indeed, so many people would like a college education but can't afford it. They are completely shut out of the picture.

While most institutional leaders blame changing demographics or lack of funding for low enrollment, a more important issue is at stake: the disconnect between what a college education offers and what young people need to launch lucrative careers in the twenty-first century. Let's look at it this way: every business exists to provide a solution to a problem, and if they aren't addressing their customers' problems properly, the product or services being offered need to change—or they'll be out of business. Low college enrollment is really because higher ed isn't offering the right solution at the right price.

CRISIS #5: STUDENTS QUESTION THE VALUE OF A COLLEGE DEGREE

"Is a college degree worth my time and money?" This is the question more and more high school graduates are asking themselves.

The aforementioned EDGE findings point us back to our opening question: "Why learn?"

The respondents of that same survey indicated that they find college important for facilitating career progression along with earning more money and having job security.

Interestingly, knowledge gain and application, life preparation, and skill development ranked much lower in their reason to get a college degree. In other words, a college degree is a means to an end. In students' eyes, having a credential on a piece of paper is worth more than actually learning. But employers want the opposite.

Young people struggle with the balancing act of weighing the cost of a college degree (and the risk of going into debt) with the value of a degree. This uncertainty can defer their enrollment for years, if not scare them away entirely. In addition, 40 percent of high school students indicated they don't even enjoy school, so why sign up for another four years of boredom and stress (Edge Research 2024)? Ouch! This is a major problem that can be turned around if higher ed is willing to break out of their mold.

When high school students and young adults ask me for advice on where to attend college, what to major in, or whether or not it's worth the investment, I have mixed feelings. As someone who deeply values education and learning and earned three degrees myself, how can I tell someone not to invest in themselves through higher education? After dealing with the realities of student loan debt, personally experiencing the lack of change in higher education from multiple perspectives, and understanding how fast our world is changing, I am inclined to suggest they consider alternative paths in building a career.

Obviously professions such as medicine, law, and accounting require specific degrees, so let's set those aside. I am referring to the 20 to 50 percent of high school students who enroll in college but haven't a clue why or what they want to study. And that's okay, because those four years are a great opportunity to discover what interests you. But according to a 2024 *Bloomberg* article, about 52 percent of college graduates are categorized as "underemployed." In other words, they are working at jobs that don't even require a college degree; therefore, they aren't even leveraging what they learned in college (Maglione 2024). Epic fail on our part.

When it comes to graduate degrees, I also question a person's reasoning for doing so. Grad school used to be a great option when the economy was in a slump or you wanted to make a significant career change, but it's a pretty expensive way to spend one to two years if you don't have a specific goal in mind or know whether a graduate degree is going to open the right doors for you. When asked for my guidance on this topic, I am inclined to tell people to get hands-on work experience instead of a graduate degree. Even MBAs are a dime a dozen these days. Remember: skills trump diplomas.

Is this their fault or the fault of a system that has failed them? Next generation learners are weighed down by financial concerns, unsure of the ROI of education investments. The lack of the joy of learning, high stress, and uncertainty about future directions form the triad of forces keeping our teenagers out of higher education. Not surprisingly, they are asking, "Why does the value of a two-year or four-year degree outweigh the value of credentials and job training programs?" And this questioning is only reinforced by hiring companies devaluing traditional academic degrees.

CRISIS #6: EMPLOYERS QUESTION THE VALUE OF A COLLEGE DEGREE

Every year, countries are ranked on who has the most highly skilled and productive workforces. The United States consistently ranks in the top ten to fifteen, whether the source is US-centric, such as US News & World Report or the Office of Economic Development, or international, such as the International Institute for Management Development in Switzerland, known for their global business research. That's the good news. But before we rest on our laurels, it is important to look a bit deeper inside organizations to understand the challenges and constraints related to professional development and upskilling. Again, there is a bigger story here.

It is important to note that people aren't saying *learning* isn't a worthwhile investment, but the traditional college experience is questionable. The formal degree pathway isn't the only way to gain marketable skills. We have so many ways to access knowledge in the information age we live in. Bootcamps, online learning platforms, self-directed learning programs, even apprenticeships offer more affordable and relevant learning opportunities that lead to well-paying jobs and launching lucrative careers.

Interestingly, a growing trend in the United States reflects that more and more companies are no longer requiring a four-year college degree to be eligible for entry-level positions. Why? Because companies need skills more than diplomas. The education system has failed them, and they realized they could find highly skilled talent from every corner of the globe—many of whom have never stepped foot on a college campus.

Leading companies such as Google, Walmart, Bank of America, Home Depot, Apple, IBM, Starbucks, Whole Foods, Hilton, and Nordstrom no longer require a college degree to be considered for employment. And the list grows every year. As a matter of fact, according to a November 2023 survey conducted by Intelligent, nearly half of eight hundred companies surveyed say they plan to eliminate bachelor's degree requirements for some positions in 2024. Lest we think this just pertains to entry-level positions, it is important to note that of the 55 percent of the employers who are axing bachelor's degree requirements, this is also the case for mid-level and senior-level roles (2024). That, my friends, is a significant signal and reinforces my point that employers value experience over education.

CRISIS #7: IRRELEVANT ASSESSMENTS
Assessments are meant to test the mastery of a topic or skill. Right? Dietel, Herman, and Knuth define assessment as "any method used to better understand the current knowledge that a student possesses" (2003). That said, some people (including me) believe that assessment and testing are not one in the same.

> While testing is formal and often standardized, assessment is based on a collection of information about what students know and what they are able to do. In other words, students are given the exact procedures for administering and scoring in testing. In assessment, on the other hand, there are multiple ways and methods of collecting information at different times and contexts (Law and Eckes 1995, 29).

The focal point of testing and assessment seems to be efficiency—fast, easy, and economical to score. Unfortunately, they don't get to the heart of learning, i.e., knowing whether learners are confident in their knowledge, as well as the ability to apply it. I understand why standardized tests were created, but they are missing the mark. What these tests are really measuring is recognition and recall, but not analysis, synthesis, and efficacy.

Too often, the assessments used in education or corporate settings focus on a standardized, single-occasion, and timed exercise meant to compare large population groups in terms of their theoretical understanding. Consider the SAT or compliance training where your score supposedly demonstrates competency. In both these formats, multiple choice questions may measure knowledge gain, but not practical application.

Take an ethics test as another example. Many companies require new employees to take an ethics test as part of their onboarding process. Typically, the employee reads about a scenario and is then presented with questions pertaining to how he or she would react in said situation. Without putting an employee in an actual situation where they feel what it's like to make a difficult or ethical decision, these assessments are largely hypothetical and therefore useless.

CRISIS #8: LAG IN ADOPTING AND ADAPTING

A big part of our current education crisis comes down to the absence of agility. Remember the Sisyphean boulder? Most learning professionals are mired in such systemic inertia that they don't even bother trying to budge that boulder up the hill. From our experiences, we have no real incentive or support to be innovative in higher education. Most faculty at four-year institutions are rewarded for publishing articles in top-tiered academic journals. This is how you earn tenure and job security. But that system doesn't have anything to do with the learner experience or outcomes or innovation. Undoubtedly, individual champions exist here and there, but very few institutions are systematically drivers of change, thanks in part to deep-seeded bureaucracy.

What positions some institutions to be more innovative than other institutions? Is it money? Is it leadership? Is it access to other resources? I believe it comes from the top. They have leaders who are visionary and open minded. These institutions can *adapt* to change without missing a beat and *adopt* new ways of thinking and teaching that will steamroll other institutions.

Sometimes it begins with a great leader building a strong foundation. Take Dr. Michael Baston, president of Cuyahoga Community College (Tri-C) in Ohio as an example. When he was first hired at Tri-C, one of the first matters at hand was to put together his new executive team. "I did not hire lots of higher ed people with higher ed degrees and higher ed backgrounds. I hired people from the community with information, with relationships, and with expertise to inform higher ed and to make us stronger and better." Now that's how you break out of the status quo.

ADAPTING

a·dapt
/əˈdapt/

Make (something) suitable for a new use or purpose; modify. Become adjusted to new conditions.

Whether we like it or not, we are nudged to adapt to new ways of being all the time. It's human evolution and growth. It might not be easy or always make sense at first, especially when faced with pronounced uncertainty, but it is part of life. External forces are usually out of our control (can you say "pandemic," anyone?) and can force us to adapt to a new normal.

As learning leaders, we are not immune from change. As a matter of fact, given our role of preparing young people for their lives and careers, doesn't it make sense that we should be the ones leading the change to help our learners better manage change and disruption? The benefit of a few for maintaining the status quo cannot and should not override the potential benefits to millions of students and future employees. We really need to *expect* and *embrace* new conditions from outside the walls of the academy to best serve our learners. And this is not a one-and-done proposition. We should be in a constant state of change—and most people don't want to hear that. An additional challenge comes from managing the increased pace of change. No sooner have we introduced online learning and Zoom sessions than they are outdated by AI or the next technology hurtling around the corner at us.

ADOPTING

a·dopt
/əˈdäpt/

Choose to take up, follow, or use. Formally approve or accept.

Adopting new things, such as technology or even new ways of thinking or living, takes time and effort. It doesn't happen overnight and requires a well-thought-out plan. Consider moving your family to a new country with a different language and culture. Acculturation takes time and is usually faced with resistance until the new becomes the norm. (Heck, I experienced a bit of culture shock when I moved from Fairfield County, Connecticut, to New York City back in 1997.)

Adopting something new requires us to unlearn something we have learned in the past and have accepted as truth or the best option or what we're most comfortable with, and then open our minds to relearn. This process is based on the Cycle of Unlearning. I came across an article entitled "Learn Unlearn Relearn: Breaking the Cycle of Failure in Education" on EducateMe (Shauk 2025). It is a fascinating read.

As illustrated on the next page, the learn, unlearn, relearn theory is "a cycle of gaining and applying knowledge, discarding out-of-date information, and gaining new information that builds upon and updates the previous knowledge" (Shauk 2025). What stands out to me is the need to get rid of outdated information to in turn have breakthroughs to learn something new and more relevant. Whether we're talking about your basement, your desk, or your brain, you need to remove clutter to make room for something else. Right? *This* is what is missing in higher education. Ironic for an industry that exists to educate.

The Cycle of Unlearning In A Nutshell

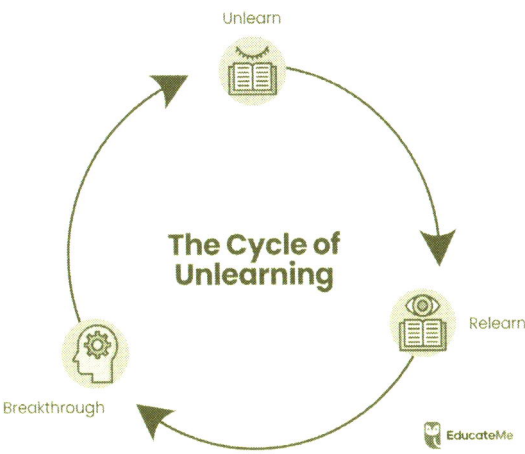

Your "why" for adopting something new should also be clear to you and to others you are bringing along for the ride. Novelty excites some people but scares others. To me, the act of adopting something new is akin to lifelong learning. There will always be something new to learn, to try, to consider in both our personal and professional lives. Wow! Sign me up. Why would I ever want to stop learning and growing and evolving?

SO WHAT? NOW WHAT?
Rather than scratching our heads and internalizing all this data as a nihilistic death wish, let's approach the situation as a crossroads or a turning point at which we can do something

positive to rectify the situation. The crisis in higher education is akin to the climate change crisis. We can see the impact of our negligence. Endless statistics and data points beg for change. We are continuously warned about the looming negative impacts of our actions and the implications if we don't change our mindsets and behavior. Yet it perplexes me that so many people turn a blind eye. The worst course of action in both scenarios is doing nothing.

Continuing to kick the can down the road results in loss for learners and organizations. Those who stand to benefit from maintaining the status quo of existing systems and structures, traditional teaching/training methods, and more are the incumbents. Plenty of people in higher education benefit from retaining old ways of doing, thinking, and being, and thus have no interest in changing, even though change is critical for young students and employees. Matt Alex of Beyond Academics strongly believes that the incumbents within the systems and bureaucracies of higher education are to blame for their quicksand-like foundation. "Everyone thinks the same way. So if everyone in the room looks the same, speaks the same, dresses the same, thinks the same, and you're asking for a change? That won't happen, right? They don't know anything better. They don't understand what is different."

Here's our challenge: We can no longer prepare people for careers or workplaces or lives that have existed for decades. Even preparing them for careers or workplaces or lives of *today* is missing the mark. We need to be educating people for an unknown future; for jobs that don't yet exist; for industries that are about to disappear and what will replace them; for new skills that have not yet been developed. Do you see the shift? If we as educators don't adapt, our learners and employees will be ill-prepared. Period. It is *our* responsibility to adapt to best serve our audience so they, too, are able to adapt. If we don't change, eventually our positions and institutions will have no value. What's at stake is a loss of money, time, talent, and opportunity for multiple generations.

To create or alter a system whereby the entire organization is on board with a nontraditional learning environment and experience is not an easy feat. Honestly, I think it is easier to create a new entity than to drive change from within an organization that might be set in its ways. This holds true for any industry that is ripe for change. Here's a perfect example:

> The first yellow taxi cabs in New York City hit the streets in 1897. In 1937, New York City's mayor at the time, Fiorello LaGuardia, signed the Haas Act, which was the beginning of the medallion system that still exists today. Only so many medallions can be issued (today that number is around 12,000 to 13,000), which means the number of legal yellow taxi cabs in operation in the city is limited.
>
> The price of a taxi medallion has fluctuated dramatically over the years peaking at $800,000 in 2012, dipping down to $79,000 in 2021, and latest figures indicate a price of $137,000 today. The point is: The number of taxis were—and still are—limited, while the population in New York City continued to grow. Today, about eight million people live in the five boroughs. (If you want to hear some horror stories about not finding

a cab in the rain or stressing out about finding a cab on the street corner with your luggage to get to the airport on time, talk to a New Yorker.)

Now, this could be a story about supply and demand or scarcity, but I'm going down a different rabbit hole. It's called complacency. Regardless of the amount of people living in NYC, what changed in our world was technology and new ways of living. The New York City Taxi and Limousine Commission became very complacent, feeling they had a hold on the market.

Fast forward to 2009 with the introduction of Uber, followed by Lyft in 2012. As with any entrepreneurial venture, it comes down to addressing a big, hairy problem with a new, value-add solution. The founders of Uber were visionaries and problem solvers and completely disrupted the taxicab industry, not just in New York City but worldwide. They focused on the customer experience—the convenience of having a car on demand, transparency on pricing *before* getting into the car, the ability to communicate with drivers, GPS maps to know exactly where they were going, the ability to share ride details with others, safety features, and more.

Unfortunately, the players of the existing ecosystem—especially the taxicab owners—were so narrow minded and complacent that they would have never instilled such change. The change had to come from outside the system with the introduction of something totally new. Indeed, it's not just about creating something new; it is about addressing a problem that customers have.

The entry of Uber and Lyft, followed by other taxicab alternatives, have left traditional cab companies in the dust. The incumbents are scratching their heads wondering how this happened and scrambling to compete in the market they once dominated. Traditional cab companies will likely become extinct in the very near future. Customers have found a better alternative. This is what happens when we don't pay attention to the evolution of things around us. I can't help but see this same story playing out in the world of higher education.

Now, before we can learn how to address this big crisis before us, it is imperative we unlearn some things. Easy? No. Possible? Yes. The caveat is that learning or unlearning isn't just an exercise of knowledge in, knowledge out. Feelings, experiences, beliefs, belonging, and more are intertwined with what we believe to be true. Perceptions and values may need to be tweaked. Behaviors may need to be altered.

Per Dr. Chris Dede of the Harvard Graduate School of Education, "It's harder to change if you have to unlearn something. A lot of what happens is people say, 'I'm going to teach you this transformative thing that you're going to do,' and it's all cognitive. And then they wonder why nothing happens. Well, unlearning involves social support and affected support, because you're giving up part of your identity without a clear idea of what the new identity is going to be."

Are you ready to *unlearn*?

CHAPTER 4

The Buffet

INFORMATION OVERLOAD

When you hear the word "buffet," does it bring up feelings of excitement and abundance? Or do you feel anxious and overwhelmed? I'm in the latter camp. I despise buffets, especially the classy all-you-can-eat version. The mere thought of a buffet makes me instantly have a stomachache. It's like a license to gorge yourself for a couple of hours. You have to ensure you get your money's worth, so you pile your plate high, go back for seconds or even a (gasp!) third round of helpings. Then, as stuffed as you are, you just can't pass up that dessert table now, can you? *What is up with that?*

> *Fun facts: Early origins of the buffet can be traced back to the Swedes and the French, but leave it to Americans to take it over the top. The concept of the all-you-can-eat buffet was introduced by Herbert Cobb McDonald in 1946 in Las Vegas (Blitz 2017).*

I equate this overabundance of food with the overabundance of information we are privy to today. On one hand, we want more, more, more! But it's all too much, and many of us feel like we can't possibly keep up with all the information being thrown at us by the media, and yes—educators. As subject-matter experts and educators, we have been programmed to share our knowledge and expertise with our learners. Before the internet, the sage on the stage had real value.

We are deeply into the Information Age that technically began in the mid-twentieth century. With respect to learning, we as scholars and disseminators of knowledge have to keep reminding ourselves that we *all* have access to unlimited amounts of information, 24-7, *for free*. So why do learners need us? Why do they cough up time and money to learn from teachers/trainers? No, really... think about that. What value are we adding to the e-books, articles, blog posts, research reports, videos, news bites, tutorials, etc. to which learners already have access? More importantly, what are we doing to help our learners understand what to do with all this information overload?

FROM KNOWLEDGE TO INTELLIGENCE AND EXPERIENCE
World-renowned management consultant Peter Drucker coined the term "knowledge worker" in the original 1959 version of his book, *The Landmarks of Tomorrow*. Drucker defined knowledge workers as high-level workers who acquire knowledge through formal training and then apply theoretical and analytical concepts to develop products and services. Drucker's concept made ripples in the 1950s as he questioned why knowledge needed to be abstract, and instead touted experience as the cornerstone of knowledge necessary for the "postmodern" era of work. The knowledge worker's role, then,

was to identify pattern, purpose, and process in the experiences they encountered. Drucker acknowledged the seismic shift facing 1950s learning organizations: "Ours is the first society in which 'honest work' does not mean a callused hand. This is […] a change in the human condition" (Drucker 1996).

In 2025, what signifies "honest work"? Certainly not only the callused hand of blue-collar workers or the spectacled brow of knowledge workers. It is the synthesis of head, hearts, and hands we referred to when describing education reforms by Montessori, Dewey, and others in a previous chapter. Whether you are a factory operator learning about manufacturing electric vehicle batteries using augmented reality, or a car salesperson using e-learning to learn how to showcase car features, or an automotive executive working with international, cross-functional teams to engineer and design concept cars, we are making sense of our professional worlds using multiple senses: verbal, logical, spatial, interpersonal.

COVID-19 threw another curveball at us. In the post-pandemic era, work is no longer a place you go to but a role employees can perform from anywhere and even any time. Dr. Karen Linkletter, writing about the new post-knowledge worker, points out that knowledge work was motivating in and of itself and encouraged organizational efficiency to the detriment of culture and people. In the 2020s, our collective shift away from a "hustle culture" to prioritizing work/life balance and purpose-based work means we need employees and students to develop "fusion competence" (Linkletter, 2024). We must learn how to balance analytical, emotional, and practical skills in tandem, sort of like a masterful fusion chef.

Look at how much has changed since the turn of the century, with machine learning and artificial intelligence (AI) training systems helping us process and analyze vast amounts of information and data. As we begin to equip our students and colleagues for the future of work, we need to acknowledge that the new "landmarks of tomorrow" include human-machine collaboration, experience, and creativity. With the help of AI, we can create personalized, engaging, immersive experiences for learners. This is not something to fear.

The World Economic Forum reports that we are in our fourth Industrial Revolution. We are actually in the midst of transitioning from the Information Age to the Intelligent Age. "The Intelligent Age—driven by rapid advancements in artificial intelligence (AI), quantum computing and blockchain—is transforming everything and changing it right now, in real time" (2024). So now, it's not just a matter of accessing an abundance of information. It's what we are able to do with all of that data to make more intelligent decisions. Yes, AI is disrupting essentially every aspect of our lives, but it is also opening up countless opportunities. Just keep in mind that AI doesn't learn for us; that must be a personal experience.

In addition, the Age of Experience is also evolving around us. Not only can we access and analyze information in mind-blowing ways, but we can also *experience* it thanks to immersive technologies. This shift is challenging us to rethink how humans, machines, and the combination of the two are processing information.

> With the rise of the metaverse and virtual worlds, the line between the digital and physical is becoming increasingly blurred. Virtual spaces are emerging

where people can work, socialize and even own digital assets—ushering in new forms of economic and social interaction (WEF 2024).

Going forward, immersive experiences will be more important, and definitely more engaging, than simple knowledge gain (Bennet 2019). Seriously—wouldn't it be more fun to be immersed in a game or movie as an active participant instead of a passive observer?

JUGAAD: SCARCITY-DEFYING INNOVATION

Growing up during the 1980s and 1990s in a country where buffets and abundance were a rarity, Yogini often recalls a distinct passion that fueled her and her peers: the hunger for knowledge and the conviction that education and skills were the ticket to progress and prosperity. The buffets that she remembers are those feeding the mind and brain, from a high school where six hundred students and sixty teachers shared one single computer to achievements garnered in spite of a lack of access to resources. Indeed, being hungry leads to greater innovation and achievement compared to being overwhelmed with buffet options. This belief sustains the Indian practice of *jugaad*.

Jugaad is a Hindi word that loosely translates to "the gutsy art of overcoming harsh constraints by improvising an effective solution using limited resources" (Radjou et al. 2011). *Jugaad* is a "bottom-up" innovation approach that provides organizations in both emerging and developed economies the key capabilities they need to succeed in a fast-moving, hyper-competitive world. *Jugaad* is an antidote to pervasive scarcity, relying on three main practices: rapid prototyping, frugal innovation, and a razor-sharp focus on adaptable and inclusive solutions.

Navi Radjou and company broke new ground in 2011 with their article published in the *Harvard Business Review* that proposed the *jugaad* mindset is relevant for companies worldwide seeking to grow in an increasingly complex and resource-constrained business environment. Unlike traditional, structured innovation methods that rely on time-consuming and expensive R&D processes, the more fluid *jugaad* approach delivers speed, agility, and cost efficiencies.

Consider the case of Dr. Lakshmi Saleem, one of the first female plastic surgeons in India. Unlike her Western counterparts who might serve vanity or appearance through plastic surgery, Dr. Saleem uses her medical skills to treat burn victims, mainly Indian women suffering from domestic violence. She humbly states, "I have learned plastic surgery from my patients. Necessity became the mother of invention." Without access to advanced resources, she has thought nimbly mid-surgery to use parts of wire clothes hangers to suture skin and shifted focus from beautification to survival with dignity (Saleem 2018). Talk about rapid prototyping, frugal innovation, and adaptable and inclusive solutioning!

From an educator's perspective, *jugaad* teaches us we don't need a buffet of resources to bring innovation into our classrooms and workplaces. We need to accept that to succeed in a fast-moving world with high competition for learners' attention, we need to practice frugality, not abundance. Time is a valuable resource both for educators and learners. We need to practice inclusivity and collaboration, trying to view knowledge and skills from the learners' perspective. That will be the new twist to the "flipped classroom" where teachers learn from their students as much as the other way around. Above all, we need to pay attention to our learners' needs and desires to get their attention.

From a learner's perspective, sitting in a classroom-style environment, consuming somebody else's recipe on what to know, do, or think, and then regurgitating it back is stifling, not satisfying. For learners in universities and companies, *jugaad* can be liberating. It's simultaneously a challenge to problem solve and figure out the best solutions with the least amount of resources and an invitation to share responsibility for learning. It can also instill a hunger for learning, which over time fuels a lifelong learning mindset.

WHAT ARE ADULT LEARNERS HUNGRY FOR TODAY?

To truly understand adult learners and their needs, it's helpful to refer to adult learning theory, or andragogy, which is accredited to Malcolm Knowles. Let's have a refresher. His adult learning theory model posits that adult learners not only want to understand *what* they are learning, they want to know *why*. Adults prefer to learn by doing—through personal experience—and build upon what they have already experienced and learned throughout the process.

> **Knowles' Four Principles of Andragogy (Pappas 2023)**
>
> 1. Adults need to be involved in the planning and evaluation of their instruction.
> 2. Experience (including mistakes) provides the basis for the learning activities.
> 3. Adults are most interested in learning subjects that have immediate relevance and impact to their job or personal life.
> 4. Adult learning is problem-centered rather than content-oriented.

Great. This was developed in the 1980s. Is it still relevant today? Well, here's what adult learners want in this day and age, according to articles about adult learners by Buglione and Billups (2023) and ELM Learning (2022):

1. Adults consider time their most precious commodity. They, therefore, want learning to be relatively quick, convenient, and relevant.

2. While collaboration is omnipresent in our professional lives, many adult learners prefer to learn on their own, at their own pace. Again, they don't want other people wasting their precious time.

3. Adult learners appreciate a sense of community and support, as well as a safe space to speak freely, debate, experiment, and make mistakes.

4. They want to learn things that are relevant to them personally and support their personal career goals.

5. Adults tend to be goal-oriented and want to see the fruits of their labor. They want to see a clear benefit for the time they carved out for learning.

6. Adults can be set in their ways, so introducing new skills or technologies needs to be supported with rationale and change management strategies.

In addition to this, we also should keep in mind that young professionals today—those digital natives—have additional expectations, as reported by Training Industry (Teo 2023).

1. They expect learning to be more personalized or customized to their personal needs, professional goals, and pace of learning.

2. They prefer experiential learning: hands-on activities with tangible outcomes versus passive learning sessions.

3. They expect to utilize the latest technology in the workplace and for learning, because this is how they operate all the time. Mobile apps, gamification, and emerging technologies will keep these learners engaged.

4. Like accessing the news, young professionals prefer to learn in small, bite-sized pieces. Micro-learning is popular with this generation and seems to help with knowledge retention.

5. They expect any learning or new skill development to have purpose and be clearly linked to real-world application.

6. Collaborative learning is attractive to them because they value diversity and varying perspectives.

7. Experiential learning with practical application keeps this generation (with short attention spans) engaged and motivated.

8. Leveraging various forms of media, such as videos and simulations, are preferred to reading piles of documents.

9. Regular—and personable—feedback, mentorship, and recognition will keep learners motivated and inspired.

Wow! How do we keep up with that? Well, not only do our teaching methods and modes need to change, but so do the resources, experiences, and activities we utilize. How we share information and our expertise now should be in alignment with how learners expect and want to acquire, utilize, share, and experience knowledge and skills. This is a noteworthy shift in the dynamics between educators and learners.

KEEPING THINGS FRESH
Although the exact age range is debatable, generally speaking, anyone born between 1980 and 2000 is considered a digital native as well as a millennial (Akçayir et al. 2016). Frankly, anyone born since then is by default a digital native. In 2023, millennials and Gen Zers made up nearly 40 percent of the

workforce. I've seen various predictions as to how this number will grow over time, but the point is that within the next few years, this group of digital natives will be the dominant generation in the workplace. Dr. Jia Wang, a professor in the Department of Educational Administration and Human Resource Development at Texas A&M University, published an article entitled "Understanding a Multigenerational Workforce." She predicted that millennials will account for three-quarters of the global workforce by 2025 (Wang 2024). Yowza!

Twenty years ago, being tech-savvy meant you knew how to use the Microsoft Office Suite of tools. Now, being tech-savvy has evolved exponentially and is more than just knowing how to use the latest productivity tools and applications. The younger generations are more accustomed to building things such as websites, digital marketing materials, and algorithms. They also have more interest in understanding how things work behind the scenes and how to troubleshoot (Thompson 2023). This links to their desire to be self-sufficient and resourceful. And they want answers with the snap of a finger.

Another article entitled "Understanding Today's Generational Differences in the Workforce and Technological Preferences" from *Firm of the Future* paints an interesting picture of younger, tech-savvy generations and how they prefer to work: "They naturally expect workplace technologies to mirror the technologies they use in their educational and personal experiences" (Wiley 2020). They are hyperconnected, all the time. Growing up with ever-evolving technology, they *expect* change and are thus much more agile than older generations.

They not only expect change, but they are also change agents themselves (Thompson 2023).

Of particular note is that mobile devices are seen as a personal extension of millennials and Gen Zers and thus a necessity in life. They often arrive to work with their earbuds in and work throughout the day with them in. This is a good indicator they would welcome training via podcasts and other audio formats. Granted, mobile devices aren't the best tools for learning, depending on the subject matter, but my point is that if you were born before 1980, you learned in a much different way. Imagine how different your life was then versus how people lived in the 1940s. Taking that into context, put yourself in the shoes of younger students and employees as they live and work *today*.

This leads me to think of "learning in the flow of work," a paradigm introduced by human resources authority Josh Bersin back in 2018. Bersin is recognized in the industry as a leading subject matter expert in corporate learning, talent management, and human resources. The following chart is from an article he wrote entitled "A New Paradigm for Corporate Training: Learning in the Flow of Work" and showcases how corporate training has evolved since the late 1990s (Bersin 2018). Note where we were in 2018 when this was published; we are well into learning in the flow, which is essentially where people learn on the fly, when they need it, in a convenient format that is short and concise.

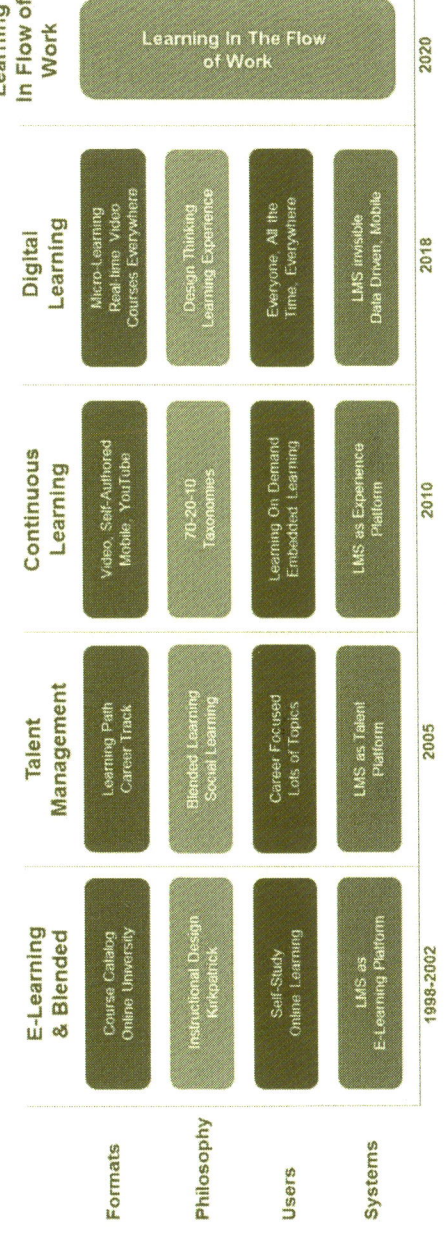

Because employees want access to information and answers to problems in real time, it makes sense to enable them to use technology tools and devices they are comfortable with. That said, not everyone wants to consume all their learning on a smartphone, and not all learning activities are best delivered this way, but it is an option that L&D professionals should consider as they adapt their own learning experiences.

Flow theory in psychology describes a state in which people are so involved in an activity that nothing else seems to matter. The concept originates from Mihaly Csikszentmihalyi, who explains, "The best moments in our lives are not the passive, receptive, relaxing times… The best moments usually occur if a person's body or mind is stretched to its limits in a voluntary effort to accomplish something difficult and worthwhile" (Oppland 2016). While designing learning in the flow of work, learning professionals should strive to create content that stretches minds to the limits, and provides a sense of accomplishment and worth. *We* need to stretch ourselves to the limit to experiment boldly and not be complacent with the same old.

Where are you on this continuum? Ideally, we should all be falling off the right-hand side of the chart.

Even though this concept is targeted at learning in the workplace, it is indicative of how college-level young adults want to learn. Sure, learning in the flow of work happens during internships or apprenticeships, but it can also be translated into experiential learning in college classrooms. Rather than bombarding students with excess information, consider more microlearning or project-based work whereby they pick up new skills and knowledge while they're in the flow of researching something or trying to solve a problem.

SO WHAT? NOW WHAT?

The takeaway here is that the learner and educator interplay has been in a state of disruption since well before the turn of the century. The profusion of information available to learners demands we adapt our roles as holders and disseminators of key information to be more like tech-savvy facilitators, guides, and mentors that support learners in their own personal self-discovery and learning by doing.

Learning just to gain knowledge or understand a theory is no longer sufficient in our world. Learners need to learn the very latest in technology to take advantage of the greater intelligence afforded them. They are capable of learning at a deeper level and thinking at a much higher level—given the opportunity to expand beyond a prescribed menu. Such skills and knowledge and experiences will give them power and strength.

To that end, our responsibility to learners should look more like this:

- Help them winnow down vast amounts of information and confirm what's valid and accurate.

- Strengthen their analytical skills based on data, data, data.

- Lead them to make the best use of what machine learning and artificial intelligence can bring to their daily study and work routines.

- Help them make sense of knowledge and information through experience.

- Teach them to be agile and open minded.

- Help them build confidence in making decisions even with limited information and resources at hand using the *jugaad* mindset.

- Create just-in-time microlearning tools to support learning in the flow.

Hanover Research published a report in March 2024 highlighting how the graduating Gen Z and the incoming Gen Alpha care about agency and choice (2024). We, too, often constrain ourselves and our learners to an experience akin to a toddler's plastic plate with dividers. You get a specific amount of this, this, and this. No choices. No going outside the dividers. It's prescribed. Mealtime becomes predictable and boring.

One more thing: Humans consume food for sustenance and to stay alive. Humans similarly consume information for mental and cognitive stimulation and growth. In both cases, what is being consumed is essentially fuel to expend energy. In the case of information, that simply means we should *do* something with all that knowledge in meaningful ways. Our brains have the ability to handle the overabundance of information. We just need to learn how to better manage how it is consumed and applied.

CHAPTER 5

D) None of the Above

Quick quiz:

What is the most effective way to measure learning outcomes?

A) Multiple choice tests
B) Cumulative exams
C) PowerPoint presentations
D) None of the above

Learning isn't a one-size-fits-all proposition, so wouldn't it make sense that learner assessments follow the same protocol? Unfortunately, these direct measures are some of the most common tools used to assess learner progress. Whether the learning occurs in a face-to-face setting or online, all too often the culmination of said learning ends with measuring how well learners memorize or parrot back information. Granted this isn't always the case, but we see such types of assessment everywhere, from communications courses to ethics and compliance tests.

I'll give in a little bit here and admit that sometimes such assessments can confirm if someone *understands* a subject, but the measures don't necessarily capture whether someone truly learned or will retain that information long-term, or that they can *apply* the knowledge or skill. What we should be utilizing are more relevant, authentic assessments if we want to ensure learners are actually learning.

An accurate and holistic assessment of a learner's "learning experience" can be time consuming, so most teachers and trainers utilize quick and easy assessment tools. Unfortunately, this also impacts how learning goals, objectives, and outcomes are developed, because learners are being assessed on superficial levels of understanding or their memorization and recall abilities. In school, learners are focused more on getting a passing grade on a standardized test versus deep learning. But that's how the education systems have groomed them.

As professors in higher ed, we primarily measure knowledge gain, with some focus on application and problem solving through assessments. When our graduates get to the workplace, they are stumped when faced with differing assessment criteria. Performance reviews are not focused on how much information employees gain or retain. They are focusing on key performance indicators related to the job—whether it is sales targets or process efficiency or innovation or teamwork. A colleague recently shared the story of a medical student who bombed his Ivy League hospital surgery placement test because he studied to the nth degree on medical knowledge, definitions, and jargon.

How do we know learners are actually learning? What *should* we be measuring?

LEARNER-CENTRIC ASSESSMENT

Whether it is course grades or employee appraisals, the assessment process is usually a one-way street. Those with authority (instructors or managers) are rating those without authority (students and employees). While this might seem normal, when a person's progress is reduced to a one-way report that is often whittled down to a number or letter, we're missing a good portion of the story, including the nuances of growth and efficacy.

One of the first steps we can take is to shift the assessment equation to zero in on the learner's needs. It begins with learner-centric curriculum design but then needs to carry through to the assessment piece. This can have a huge impact on learner motivation, engagement, and confidence, which solidifies the entire learning process. We want both positive outcomes and a positive experience with the assessment itself.

Plenty of research reinforces many of the benefits of learner-centric assessment. Of note are findings from Duncan and Buskirk-Cohen's research recorded in their article "Exploring Learner-Centric Assessment" in the *International Journal of Teaching and Learning in Higher Education*.

> Learner-centered assessment brought fun back into the classroom. Our students reported enjoying completing their project and seeing assessment as a process, rather than just an end product. As professors, we felt enthusiasm when grading their projects, rather than a dreary sense of resignation typically experienced when evaluating exams. We were nurturing and developing lifelong learning skills in our students and giving them the confidence to use them (2011).

Years ago, Yogini was facing a dilemma while teaching a business communications course at a major Indian business school. Her contract stated that she needed to design a multiple-choice test to demonstrate that her students had grasped the material, yet she knew their test scores would not have been a true indicator of their communication competency. The students—mostly millennials—thought their communication skills were pretty good when it came to selfie videos, collaborative document writing, active engagement with texting, and emailing across peer groups. These *were not* business communications skills. Houston, we had a problem.

The prospect of talking to a live person for an internship interview or giving a live speech in front of an audience struck fear in their hearts. Yogini quickly realized that the cohort struggled with digital literacy. They didn't pay attention to whether their communication channels (texting, emailing) were appropriate for the recipient, and they also struggled with determining the right tone or language.

The choices looming before Yogini were:

1. Create a standard multiple-choice test.

2. Create an essay-based midterm which captures student understanding of communication theory.

3. Create an assignment that challenges students to move out of their comfort zones and develop much needed practical skills.

Also on the table was: Should she challenge the basic premise of how assessment was structured at the university? And (*gasp!*) risk going rogue? Which did she choose? *Ding, ding, ding!* Survey says… she went with option three. The assignment she created required students to identify a passion project that needed polished communication skills with a set of stakeholders. They had to determine proper channels, practice their new skills, and then analyze their individual communication successes and struggles.

The result? Several students successfully raised sponsorship for a TEDx event they held at the culmination of that semester. Others engaged with community-based projects that raised awareness for social issues. What she found is that students appreciated what they deemed "unconventional" assessment methods precisely because they were able to personally grapple with communication barriers and overcome them—a much more practical and useful outcome than a score on a test.

If we utilized this type of assessment more often, our learners would walk away with a deeper understanding of the subject, personal experience with practical application, and increased confidence in applying their skills. It does, however, require a little more work on the educator's side, as well as a mind shift. In an instructor-centered approach, the professor is the expert in the room and controls everything. In a learner-centric approach, professors and students work together as collaborators. Professors play more of a support role while the student takes center stage—not just with the learning process, but how they are evaluated on their success (Duncan and Buskirk-Cohen 2011).

ASSESSMENT VERSUS APPLICATION

You have likely heard this saying before:

> If you want to learn something, read about it.
> If you want to understand something, write about it.
> If you want to master something, teach it.

Statements like these suggest that by teaching someone else about X or how to do X, it must mean you are an expert or master of X. I see the rationale in this statement, but I'm not 100 percent satisfied with this explanation. Learning encompasses more than knowing or understanding. For instance, understanding the movements and techniques to dunk a basketball doesn't necessarily mean you can actually do it.

Here's another example: When I was working in higher ed, I was the director of entrepreneurship for over a decade. I had studied and conducted research on entrepreneurship as part of my doctoral program and had founded my own consulting business that served entrepreneurs while in graduate school. I had the experience and qualifications to teach entrepreneurship at a university.

What baffled me is when other professors were tapped to teach an entrepreneurship course yet had never been an entrepreneur, much less researched or written about entrepreneurship. I thought, *How can these people possibly teach others what it feels like to be an entrepreneur when they have never gone through the experience themselves?* That's a wolf in sheep's clothing if you ask me. In this case, teaching someone else about X or how to do X does not automatically mean you can actually do X.

I fall into the camp that believes that if you cannot perform the concepts you have learned, then you have not fully learned. Take a leadership development course as another example. You can learn about all sorts of tools, models, tactics, strategies, intended outcomes, and so on with respect to good leadership, but if you don't actually apply these things in a real-life situation, I beg to differ you have learned how to be a leader. This is precisely why learning by doing or experiential learning is so powerful.

Rather than have grades or transcripts or scores or checkboxes, wouldn't it be better if everyone had their own learning portfolio, much like an artist? Artists curate a physical or digital portfolio of their work to show people what their skills and talents are. Producing a diploma that one went to art school probably doesn't matter, because at the end of the day what matters is *what you can do with what you learned*.

Rather than focusing on quantifiable assessments, give learners the opportunity to demonstrate their knowledge and skills in practical ways. Without giving learners or employees agency and holding them accountable to demonstrate or apply what they learned, the result is superficial learning outcomes with low retention in the long run.

Imagine this: Everybody owns their own portfolio, and it goes with them throughout their career. It is indeed a digital portfolio, because this is the most efficient way to collect and share assets. Rather than providing a score to verify you met the baseline criteria to pass a course, you could prove your proficiency by sharing what you created or solved or developed—whether it be an Excel model, an algorithm, a video, or a marketing campaign. Having tangible proof takes away the guessing game of "does this guy really know how to code in Python?" even though it says so on his résumé.

Portfolio-based assessment originated in the 1990s through teacher education at Stanford University. It evaluates a purposeful collection of a person's work that exhibits their individual efforts, choices, progress, and achievements in one or more competence areas. In the era of ChatGPT, such authentic assessment can be one way of ensuring learner ownership and accountability for the content they present. Similarly, problem-based assessments require learners to use analytical, collaboration, and communication skills to respond to a given situation, much like the mid-term communication passion project Yogini assigned to her students.

One of the best use cases of portfolio-based assessment Yogini has seen was at the Mountbatten Institute, a not-for-profit organization that connects young professionals with top global businesses through international internships, cultural exchange, and graduate coursework. In a unique twist, the program required each participant to compete against themselves by setting personal, professional, and cultural competence goals for their twelve-month internship, and then collecting and presenting evidence of their progress toward meeting these objectives through quarterly self-assessments.

One of the shortcomings of using such alternative assessments is that they can be too subjective and, therefore, unreliable and invalid. To counter the subjectivity bias, Mountbatten learners' self-evaluation is triangulated with performance reviews from their internship managers and instructors, including a Likert scale rating of different competency areas. In the aggregate, this kind of assessment provided interns with a 360-degree picture of their strengths and areas for improvement that they could effectively leverage for transitioning from their internships to their future careers.

Luckily, we have already made a dent in adopting this holistic evaluation approach in workplaces. Employee reviews have been in place since the US military created a merit-based system during World War I to flag poor performers, according to a *Harvard Business Review* article "The Performance Management Revolution." World War I was more than a century ago. It goes without saying that merit-based performance appraisals are a last century practice that reduces creativity and accountability, increases paperwork, and destroys morale. Enter the era of talent reviews, which about 70 percent of organizations have adopted (Cappelli and Tavis 2016). The authors describe this shift:

> The biggest limitation of annual reviews—and, we have observed, the main reason more and more companies are dropping them—is this: With their heavy emphasis on financial rewards and punishments and their end-of-year structure, they hold people accountable for past behavior at the expense of improving current performance and grooming talent for the future, both of which are critical for organizations' long-term survival. In contrast, regular conversations about performance and development change the focus to building the workforce your organization needs to be competitive both today and years from now (Cappelli and Tavis 2016).

Focusing on collaborative goal setting, personal as well as professional growth, and practical application versus basic knowledge acquisition are the future of employee assessment. Organizations that adopt these practices will see increased productivity and commitment from employees. That said, we still need to make sure we are accurately tracking learner growth and performance. *How* we go about this is critical for out-of-the-box outcomes.

MODERN-DAY METRICS

Betterworks, a performance management software company, knocked out an amazing skills report in 2024 that dove into performance data. They surveyed over 1,100 people managers in the United States at companies of various sizes to understand how they assess employee performance, manage upskilling, and address skills gaps. What they discovered is there are still a lot of shortcomings and obstacles that companies face when it comes to performance measurement (2024, 4–5):

1. Lack of meaningful learner data
2. Infrequent performance evaluations
3. Absence of mentoring and coaching programs
4. Inability to identify skills gaps
5. Lag in tech adoption for skills assessment

What this tells us is that we need to capture more relevant data, more frequently, and on a deeper level. We need to provide more feedback and support on a regular basis. And we need to update our tech stack.

Acorn, a performance and learning management software company, published "Your Guide to the L&D Metrics That Matter for Proving the ROI of Learning," which is a great place to start. They identified the following key metrics that should be foundational in your organization or institution: learning engagement, training cost per employee, knowledge retention, impact of training on performance, training feedback, time to proficiency, and training ROI (2024).

I have seen similar lists from human resources and L&D organizations. Some metrics such as ROI, engagement, and training feedback are important, but some metrics still feel dated to me. Things like assessment scores and time to completion are useless in most cases. Time spent on an e-learning course and test scores are not indicators of engagement. As mentioned, the ways we capture and measure learner progress is key, and proven techniques and incredible tech tools on the market today go beyond fundamental data points and link back to the current challenges mentioned above.

MEANINGFUL LEARNER DATA

Instead of tracking whether someone watched a video and passed an online quiz, or tracking how long it took someone to complete a training session, we should focus on metrics such as increased confidence levels, true engagement levels, and an accurate demonstration of skills. For example, conducting pre- and post-surveys on confidence for a negotiation training session can tell us just how impactful the training was if learners indicate an increase in confidence in a new skill. This is a good indicator how well they will perform a task or skill when faced with the real-world situation.

Given that low engagement is omnipresent when it comes to typical learning and training, let's find out to what extent learners are really engaged with learning. This is tough to track on Zoom when people don't show their faces; and even if they do, they are probably multitasking. We see this same disconnect in face-to-face situations all the time. People are multitasking on their laptops or phones, so how do you know if they are paying attention and actually learning?

At Edstutia, we decided to walk the talk when it came to learner assessment using modern day metrics and technology. One of our unique features is a holistic dashboard that starts with learner data from our LXP, incorporating learner satisfaction and confidence metrics as well as instructor assessment of learner output during social learning and gamified knowledge retention activities. But instead of stopping at self-assessment and teacher assessment, we layer in input from the VR headset (with user permission), such as gaze tracking and audio tracking to measure learner engagement, and data from hotspots during immersive, hands-on experiences capturing learner confidence and knowledge application. *Voila!* Our learners now get a robust sense of how much they know, how confidently they can apply newly learned skills, how they show up interpersonally, and where they can develop further.

I'm still a fan of capturing learner satisfaction and feedback, which is a common post-training metric, but we need to go beyond smiley faces and Likert scales. Capturing regular feedback from our learners on an iterative level allows us to adjust our curriculum and content on the fly if need be. Qualitative feedback is way more useful than numbers in this case, so it is in our best interest to listen more than count.

MEASURING WHILE DOING

Evaluating learner progress while they are in the thick of it instead of capturing post-intervention evaluations can make all the difference with learning outcomes. Learners should regularly be able to demonstrate knowledge gain and understanding throughout the learning process. Consider how imperative this is in fields such as healthcare where there's often no room for error. In global health, the failure to translate *what is known* to *what needs to be done* with respect to patient care is an example of the "know-do gap" (Drexler 2020).

By applying a "measuring while doing" approach, real-time assessment methods during the training gauge a learner's grasp of the material through interactive quizzes, polls, and knowledge checks integrated into the training modules, allowing learners to immediately apply what they have learned. Take it a step further, and tools providing just-in-time learning while employees are performing a real-life task and assessing their performance "live" provides rich, learner-centric data and reduces the know-do gap.

A 2018 report from the Lancet Global Health Commission records how a real-time diagnostic assistance tool called UpToDate was deployed to support medical professionals while making decisions in hospital settings (Kruk and Pate 2020). The data about decision making served as the basis for measuring while doing and demonstrated that the just-in-time tool saved approximately 11,500 lives and 372,500 hospital days over a three-year period (Caron 2011).

TALENT MANAGEMENT SYSTEMS

Most organizations have a learning management system (LMS) in place to manage content, user accounts, resource sharing, and yes—learner progress. In addition to an LMS, another tool to consider is a talent management system. These are software solutions that can be integrated into your existing tech stack. The beauty is these systems manage the full range of an employee's journey—from recruitment and onboarding to L&D to succession planning. Tools like this offer a more holistic picture of each employee.

> Talent management systems focus on helping companies and HR achieve their long-term (business) goals by putting the employees—or talent, if you like—first. This means that rather than focusing on transaction processing and administration, like for instance, a traditional HRMS does, a talent management system is about building an employee-centric solution (Verlinden n.d.).

Today, the vast majority of employees (80 percent) value the opportunity to grow and be challenged at work more than a salary according to the Academy to Innovate HR (Webber 2019). If that's the case, it seems like a worthwhile investment to have the proper tools and systems in place to support such expectations. I'm not an expert in this area, but I do know that companies like Cornerstone OnDemand, SAP, and TalentSoft have software systems that are cutting edge and more data driven than most other learning management systems on the market.

xAPI

Several technological innovations have upped the ante when it comes to measuring learning effectiveness in an intelligent, personalized way. Whatfix, an enterprise software company, curated a list of eleven different assessment innovations to measure training effectiveness (Gupta 2022). One that is particularly noteworthy is Experience API (or xAPI).

Going right to the source, xAPI.com explains that "xAPI is an eLearning specification that makes it possible to collect data about the wide range of experiences a person has within online and offline training activities. xAPI's use of a shared format for both the receiving and sending of data makes the specification an ideal tool for sharing learning between multiple systems" (xAPI n.d.). A lot of LMSs tend to focus on tracking quantitative data, but xAPI allows us to aggregate learner data and experiences from all sorts of systems and environments. The emphasis is on experiences.

This technology was founded on the belief that learning happens everywhere, not just in the classroom or during an online session. Learners now have the autonomy to update their own "Learning Record Stores" with examples of their learning through a variety of modes: mobile apps, simulations, real-world activities, peer-based learning, and collaborative learning, to name a few. This is a huge improvement over SCORM-based (or sharable content object reference model) assessments, which needed to be tied to an LMS and mainly track completion rates, time spent on learning, and test scores as opposed to the broader scope of xAPIs.

One of the biggest benefits of xAPI is personalization. xAPI tells you exactly where learning is happening, powered by analytics and reporting features. By understanding how users engage with the training content, learning professionals can use data insights to improve the learning experience by helping learners focus on relevant concepts, as the rest is automatically removed from the course through real-time content editing.

ARTIFICIAL INTELLIGENCE AND PREDICTIVE ANALYTICS

Referencing the Betterworks report, we may be missing opportunities to capture learner data, but even when we do have the data, we are often unsure what to do with all of it. It can be overwhelming, but that's where emerging tech comes into play.

If you think about it, people are entering your classrooms with differing levels of understanding and experience. They have various learning styles and preferences. Some might be more conceptual or analytical, while others are visual learners or only really "get it" when they learn by doing. It should become routine to find out the starting point of your learners, present the goals and desired outcomes, and then offer them a more personalized training path. This sounds like a lot of work, but with the help of AI and predictive analytics, much of this process can be automated for individual learners.

Already on the market are AI-powered assessment and evaluation tools that you can customize with your own rubrics and criteria for learning outcomes. So, learning leaders still control what they want assessed, but AI streamlines the process and calculates results in a fraction of the time it would take otherwise. The next level is predictive analytics, which can reveal trends and patterns in training effectiveness faster than if we analyzed the data manually. This means managers and instructors can identify issues and implement solutions sooner rather than later, making data-driven decisions and optimizing learner performance. Companies like Acorn have developed comprehensive performance learning management systems to directly tie learning analytics to performance predictions (Acorn, 2025). These tools actually make performance reviews enjoyable for both talent managers and employees.

At our company, Edstutia, we are able to take our dashboard to the next level with AI. Imagine this: As a learner, you enter a VR simulation practicing a difficult conversation with an AI bot, prompt-engineered to replicate a real life scenario in a skill you need to develop—say, balancing advocacy and inquiry as a leader. As you practice the roleplay, you are performing *as if* you are in this real situation, with visual and auditory cues that require you to think on your feet and respond authentically. An AI assessment tool records and transcribes your conversation, compares your in-the-flow output to preset metrics (in this case, the ability to balance between inquiry and advocacy), and provides you with a report on what you did well and what you need to develop further.

In a recent Gates Foundation article, the author Dr. Asyia Kazmi writes,

> AI assessors can create, deliver, and score assessments in various formats, such as verbal, handwritten, and multiple choice, using natural language processing,

speech recognition, and optical character recognition to evaluate student responses and provide feedback. These assessors have been shown to improve reliability, validity, and efficiency of assessments (2024).

SO WHAT? NOW WHAT?

It should now be evident that different types of learning and objectives require different types of assessment. In some cases, traditional assessments like quizzes, tests, or presentations might be sufficient. But in most cases, we aren't actually measuring whether students or employees have actually *learned* something and, more importantly, that they can do or demonstrate what they have learned. Given all the data-centric software, structures, techniques, and emerging technology available to us today, let's leverage them to produce more comprehensive and relevant learner assessments. Here are some tips to immediately improve your assessment processes:

- Revisit your learning goals, objectives, or outcomes and how they are currently assessed—if at all. Identify where the gaps are and whether you are tracking relevant information.

- Put yourself in your learner's shoes. How would *you* like to be assessed? What would help with engagement and retention?

- Open up the conversation to learners and invite them to be involved in the assessment process with self-reporting and peer reviews or even co-designing rubrics.

- Consider the know-do gap. Is this something you can identify with? Determine where basic understanding and knowledge gain is sufficient and where people need to demonstrate capabilities. Start by addressing training situations that are most critical or costly.

- Start researching tech tools to find which ones best meet your needs and your budget. With xAPIs and the increased ability for software systems to share information, you no longer need to rely on just one platform. Customize your tech stack.

As we begin to (1) think differently about the purpose and value of assessment, and (2) utilize more contemporary tech platforms and software, I can tell you it will be quite liberating to see the results. The amount of data we are privy to is a game changer in our field. Yes, it can be overwhelming when you discover all the nitty-gritty data points we can collect, but technologies like machine learning, predictive analytics, and AI have the capability to handle all this information. Instead of being afraid of adopting some of these new technologies, realize that not only will the experience and evaluations for your learners improve, it's also going to make your job easier and—dare I say—more rewarding.

Okay, class is over. Click here for the end-of-chapter multiple-choice quiz.

Just kidding.

CHAPTER 6

Experience Is the Best Teacher

When I was about five years old, I had a little swimming incident that scarred me for the rest of my life. I was wading in a river in Colorado with my brother and slipped on a rock. I fell backward and went under. All I remember is seeing the wavy waterline and the sky above it, and lots of air bubbles in the water as I gasped for air. I was a little kid who had yet to learn how to swim properly, and I was in full-on panic mode.

Since then, I have taken swimming lessons many, many times—even as an adult—but I don't have a good relationship with open water. The anxiety takes over. Still to this day. I'm a pretty athletic person, so it's not that I can't do the strokes or kick my legs properly, but I can't breathe. My breathing gets very shallow, and I can't hold my breath for very long. My heart races with anxiety and fear. I'm overly concerned about being able to touch the side or bottom of the pool for safety.

Now, in order to ramp up my swimming skills, I could read about swimming, watch video tutorials about swimming, and analyze Olympic swimmers all day long. But I will never truly learn to swim if I don't jump into the pool myself. Emotions and feelings are associated with the act of swimming. For example, what does it feel like to be buoyant and float? What is the relationship between breathing and physical movements in the water? What emotions am I experiencing? Fear? Anxiety? Fun? Exhilaration? Embarrassment? And a swim instructor certainly wouldn't give me a multiple-choice test at the end of my swimming lessons. That wouldn't prove much of anything. I would have to demonstrate my proficiency by doing the act of swimming in the proper environment: the pool.

I share this story because it is the perfect example of the power of experiential learning. Learning by doing is the most engaging and impactful way to learn just about anything, yet passive forms of learning still prevail in most educational institutions and organizations.

PASSIVE VERSUS ACTIVE LEARNING

Think back to your own onboarding at companies or universities. You were likely sitting in a room with other new joiners and were bombarded with loads of information. This "sit and get" format is still widely used today for transferring vast swathes of knowledge. An Association for Talent Development (ATD) study shows that only 10 percent of employees in an organization are active learners—people who learn with an intention of behavior change. On the flipside, 60 percent of employees are passive learners (Emelo 2013). They might produce the right responses at the end of a training but don't actually intend to adopt the learnings or change their behavior.

This is not to diss passive learning completely, as it might be sufficient in specific cases—for instance, when absorbing a large volume of information about a client to prepare for a presentation. But extensive research has shown that adult learners retain and apply knowledge more successfully when they are actively engaged. Active learning contributes to actual learning, whereas passive learning creates a *feeling* of learning. A superstar lecturer might create that feeling of learning, but would their performance in front of the classroom actually help you in real life situations (Deslauriers et al. 2019)?

Another factor to consider when weighing the pros and cons of passive versus active learning is culture. Cultures with high power distance, where you are supposed to show respect to authority, or with high collectivism, where you don't want to stand out or ruffle feathers, might favor passive learning. A case in point is Yogini's encounter with students from Asia who, when faced with an independent opinion paper assignment, went to her and asked, "Professor, can you tell us what we should think?"

I am a huge advocate of active learning because I know from personal experience what a difference it can make in the enjoyment of learning and the outcomes. My mom is a native of Germany, and I grew up hearing German all my life. When I was younger, I couldn't understand a thing (which was a great strategy for my mom and all her German friends so none of us kids could understand what the heck they were talking about). Around the age of seven or eight, my mom gave me some introductory books on learning German vocabulary and phraseology, which was a great start.

It was fairly easy for me to learn another language early on, but it got progressively more difficult when I began taking formal German classes in middle school, which I faithfully continued through high school. All of a sudden, learning a language came down to mostly rote memorization of verb conjugation and vocabulary tests, which (*oy vey!*) was just a lot to process. This kind of passive and transaction-based learning was not intuitive and, frankly, boring. I then lost my interest in continuing to learn the language.

When I was nine and thirteen years old, I was fortunate enough to spend my summer vacation visiting my relatives in Germany. I learned more about the German language and culture in those few months than in all the years of formal training sitting in a classroom. That shouldn't be that shocking because it is common knowledge that being immersed in a culture and speaking the language in everyday conversations is the best way to learn a language. But wow—what a difference that made in how I absorbed and processed the learning experience.

At Yale University, a student-run digital magazine called the *Yale Ledger* features research and thought leadership from the greater Yale community. A recent article entitled "The Best Ways to Learn a Language According to Research" features proven, effective ways of teaching languages, backed by a variety of studies. No surprise—*immersion* rises to the top as one of the best ways to understand and speak a new language (2023). I think the only way to really grasp a new language is to speak, practice, make mistakes, get corrected, and basically solidify that understanding with context and practical application.

The authors elaborate on this and state that "immersion replicates the way we naturally learn our first language as children, making it an intuitively effective method. It emphasizes practical, everyday use of language, which tends to facilitate better, longer-lasting language retention" (2023). Perhaps of utmost importance is that immersion stimulates active learning or learning by doing, which in turn dramatically increases understanding, engagement, and retention—not to mention enjoyment.

The process of sharing knowledge is more comprehensive than just passing along information in a book or a story or a lecture. For example, the purpose of learning about history or religion or philosophy might be to simply *understand* and think about concepts or events. But when it comes to learning a new language or topics, such as developing negotiation skills or being able to manage a manufacturing line in real time, the best way to learn is by actually *doing* these things yourself. Understanding and application are two different things. One without the other is incomplete.

ELT AND LEARNING STYLES

Experiential learning theory (ELT) is broadly associated with psychologist and educational theorist David Kolb who developed it as a young professor of organizational behavior and management at the Massachusetts Institute of Technology Sloan School of Management. Back in the 1970s, his original ELT purported that learning happens in a designated process or cycle based on experiencing, reflecting, thinking, and acting—with the learner at the center of it all.

This theory has since been confirmed by James Zull, a neuroscientist and educator, who provided compelling evidence that the learning cycle aligns with the brain's natural processes for learning. In his work, particularly in *The Art of Changing the Brain*, Zull connects David Kolb's experiential learning cycle with neuroscience, demonstrating how learning is rooted in the brain's structure and function (2002). He explains that the cycle—concrete experience, reflective observation, abstract conceptualization, and active experimentation—mirrors how the brain perceives, processes, connects, and applies new information.

Kolb's work was built off of similar research and theories from preceding scholars and psychologists such as Kurt Lewin, John Dewey, and Jean Piaget—all of whom placed experience at the heart of learning. Some of their research goes back to the late nineteenth century. Clearly society has evolved significantly since then, and so have Kolb's models over the last thirty to forty years, but this early research on the value of learning by doing is still quite relevant, especially in a world that values skills over knowledge.

Related to ELT are learning styles, which are habitual preferences for how people use the learning cycle to gain knowledge and understanding. Some learners are abstract thinkers. Some are theoretical. Some are conceptual. Some are visual. Some learners favor feelings, others facts. Some are action-oriented. Some are more reflective. And there are countless combinations.

Think about the last time you purchased a new gadget. Did you first sit down and read the instruction booklet from end to end? Did you leaf through instructions quickly to get the gist of it and then tinker around and figure things out on your own? Or were you intuitive enough to throw the instruction booklet away with the packaging and simply dive in (à la "live and learn")? (Side bar: I wrote instruction booklets for small appliances at my first job after college. I refuse to read any ever again. Let me figure things out on my own.)

Kolb describes experiential learning as a process by which knowledge results from transforming experiences. People tend to grasp information in one of two ways: through concrete experience or abstract conceptualization. Then people transform that into knowledge through reflective observation and active experimentation. This process happens best in a cycle as depicted below. Because the cycle is composed of two pairs of opposite modes, we all approach this learning cycle differently.

The Experiential Learning Cycle

While everyone has preferred ways of learning, it is possible—and desirable—to learn how to leverage *all* of these modes and preferences. When we stretch ourselves to think and learn in new ways, this is when deeper learning occurs. Instead of wondering what your preferred learning styles are, you can do an assessment called the Kolb Experiential Learning Profile (KELP), which is available via the Institute for Experiential Learning (IEL).

Kolb's work is alive and well today with the support of the Institute for Experiential Learning. I spent some time speaking with Kay Peterson, the founder and CEO of IEL, to hear firsthand how her organization is leveraging ELT and sharing it with a broader audience. "We founded the Institute for Experiential Learning to empower individuals, teams, and organizations to harness the transformative power of experiential learning (EL). By embracing this approach, people can significantly enhance their effectiveness and unlock their full potential. EL helps us understand that learning extends far beyond the confines of a classroom. It is the primary method we use to navigate life: shaping how we make decisions, solve problems, think critically, collaborate, and even engage in roles like partnering and parenting. Every time we adapt, change, or grow, we are learning."

Per Peterson, IEL's mission is to help people recognize that learning is an intentional and dynamic process—one that can be deliberately mastered to boost performance, amplify learning capacity, and drive continuous growth and development.

In addition to the previous model, Kolb identified nine experiential learning styles—habitual approaches to navigating the learning cycle. These styles are not fixed traits, but are influenced by factors such as education, personality, culture, career choices, and current context. Understanding one's learning style increases self-awareness, enabling deliberate use of the entire learning process. Over time, learners can develop greater flexibility to use all nine styles, enhancing their ability to adapt and thrive in any situation.

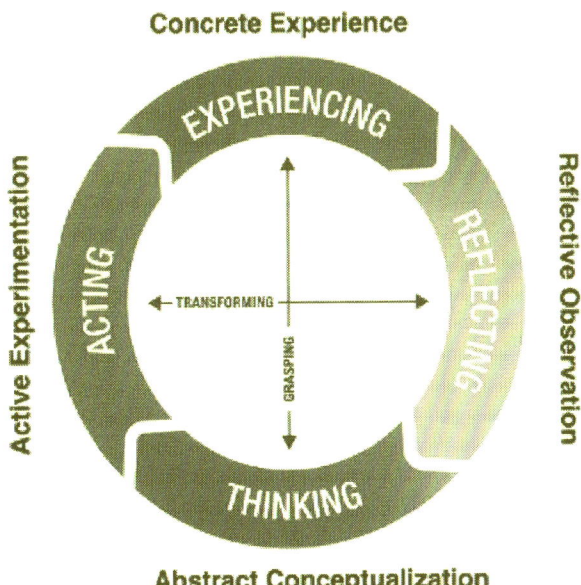

Experiential Learning Styles

As mentioned, IEL now has an assessment tool called Kolb's Experiential Learning Profile, which is, of course, based on ELT. It was designed to help individuals identify the way they learn from experience, but having this information on an individual level can be used to help people understand how they work together in teams. Understanding this dynamic can have a huge impact on organizations from a productivity standpoint because people are leveraging their strengths and using the entire process. KELP is also a great tool for educators and coaches because their learning preferences impact how they teach others. I have personally taken the KELP assessment and found it eye opening and insightful.

Understanding our learning preferences, other's learning preferences, and optimizing how we work together is super helpful and powerful. But consider this a starting point. Peterson and Kolb published a book in 2017 entitled *How You Learn Is How You Live: Using Nine Ways of Learning to Transform Your Life*. Leveraging the model above, they explain how your preferred learning styles can impact so many other aspects of our lives (2017). And when we are able to stretch or "flex" ourselves to learn in different ways, we uncover a greater potential to change and adapt.

EXPERIENTIAL LEARNING AND TEACHING STYLES

The major implication of experiential learning theory for professionals is to design training in a way that promotes deep learning for different styles. Teaching around different learning styles means that instructors need to adjust the role they have with learners—in other words, putting learners first. With this learner-centered approach, Peterson explained that educators become more than mere content experts. They adopt four roles—facilitator, expert, evaluator, and coach—to design and deliver learning experiences that foster deep, transformative learning.

Kolb's Educator Role Profile (ERP) describes four teaching styles:

Facilitator: The instructor adopts a warm affirming style to draw out learners' interests, intrinsic motivation, and self-knowledge.

Expert: The instructor adopts an authoritative, reflective style, encouraging subject matter knowledge and analysis.

Evaluator: The instructor adopts a results-oriented style, emphasizing that learners master the application of knowledge and skills.

Coach: The instructor adopts a collaborative, encouraging style, often working one-on-one with individuals to help them learn from experiences in their life context.

As learning professionals, most of us adopt all these roles to some extent; however, we tend to have preferences for certain roles. When you become aware of your preferences, you're able to make deliberate choices about what works best for you and your learners in various contexts. You're able to move your learners from merely feeling like they are learning to actually learning.

Along with becoming aware of your instructor persona, imagine tailoring learning content to these EL styles. IEL's roots lie in the 70:20:10 rule, developed in the 1980s by researchers at the Center for Creative Leadership (CCL). This rule holds that a learner absorbs 70 percent of their knowledge from on-the-job experiences. That's what experiential learning in the workplace is all about! Of the remaining 30 percent, a full 20 percent of learning happens as a result of interactions with third parties, while only 10 percent is attributable to formal learning. CCL's study found that the power of on-the-job experience is enhanced when surrounded by developmental relationships and formal learning opportunities (2022).

This same format can also be utilized in higher education or even at the high school level. I spoke with Corey Mohn, the president and executive director of CAPS Network, which is a nonprofit organization located just outside of Kansas City, Kansas, that was launched in 2021. CAPS stands for Center for Advanced Professional Studies, and they work with local high school students after their regular school day. It is similar to a career center, but the difference according to Mohn is "instead of leaning into some of the more traditional ways that vocational education has played out, that's been very much like let's drill the technical skills and then get you straight into an industry. This is more about exploration and curiosity around high school and high demand professions."

CAPS is educating the workforce of tomorrow by leveraging experiential learning, especially in high-skill, high-demand jobs. This is an opportunity outside of the formal learning structure in school for young people to gain exposure to real-world opportunities. Because the CAPS model was built to combine public education with local businesses and the local community, students are given opportunities for career exploration through highly personalized learning experiences in real-world scenarios.

Mohn explained, "Learning through curiosity, they can pick an industry that they think is interesting or maybe matches up nicely with something they like studying academically. But then they get to actually step into application and ask themselves:

Does this feel right or not feel right? And that happens in lots of different ways and ranges anywhere from just learning the basics of an industry which is relatively straightforward, but then really engaging directly with those professionals as mentors and as guest instructors, and getting offsite, and having site visits for some shadowing. The idea of working directly with these companies on challenging activities or client projects really lets them get the sense of what that industry is, what the culture is. And our purpose in doing all that is to help the students through their own self-discovery journey to play out and rule out things that don't make sense for them, which leaves them with a pool of opportunities."

WHY EXPERIENTIAL LEARNING WORKS
Why is experiential learning so beneficial to learners?

1. It is designed to engage learners' emotions.

2. It gives learners a chance to try something new, to experiment, to make mistakes, and to holistically learn from all those.

3. An active role in the learning process may give learners more agency and gratification.

4. It enables learners to connect theory with practice.

5. The added component of reflection helps learners make sense of their experiences.

6. It increases learner engagement and retention significantly.

We see this in the workplace in the form of apprenticeships. While apprenticeships have historically been associated with more blue-collar professions, having hands-on experience and relevant skills are now the hot tickets to landing well-paying jobs in growing industries. Experiential learning doesn't have to happen in a formal apprenticeship program, and it doesn't even have to happen in the workplace or in a classroom—as long as the environment and activities enable learners to be active participants in the learning process (e.g., simulations, role playing, project-based learning, even cooking), *and* they take the time to reflect on the experience.

Learning by doing can be considered somewhat of an experiment like a biology lab. By default, this can result in errors—which is a good thing. Think about a time where you nailed an exam or interview or won some sort of competition. Woohoo! That was a good feeling for sure. Now think about a time that you got a rejection letter from a prospective employer or college, for example. Ouch. That one stings. But I bet you took the time to reflect on the outcome in the latter situation compared with the first.

Sometimes it's to our detriment, but when things don't work out as planned, we reflect. We analyze. We think about what we could have done better. That reflection component of learning is critical. When things go according to plan, do you spend the time reflecting on all the things you did right? Maybe, but not with the same depth and analysis as when you fail. Experiential learning provides the exact environment needed to learn from mistakes and therefore the learning experience is that much richer, more meaningful, and stickier.

The Institute for Experiential Learning believes that EL's benefits are profound on multiple levels. From our personal experience as educators, Yogini and I are on board 100 percent. It is a powerful concept with far-reaching benefits. When you compare the time and effort to utilize EL with all the upside potential, it's a no brainer. Imagine the possibilities on all three levels:

> **For individuals**: enhanced problem-solving abilities, increased self-awareness, greater agility, improved knowledge retention, and sustained personal growth.
>
> **For teams**: strengthened collaboration, increased psychological safety, more effective knowledge sharing, reduced conflict, and innovative solutions to complex challenges.
>
> **For organizations**: accelerated innovation cycles, improved engagement and retention, and enhanced organizational learning capacity.

In 2021, *Forbes* published an article written by the Forbes Coaches Council about different ways organizations can leverage experiential learning. Some key takeaways include:

- EL helps employees take what they understand, internalize it, and apply it to real-life goals, circumstances, and challenges.

- EL raises employee's confidence in his or her abilities to perform well on the job.

- EL enables employees to be fully immersed in projects and problem solving.

SO WHAT? NOW WHAT?

An often-referenced meta-study of more than 225 separate studies of learning published in 2014 in the Proceedings of the National Academy of Sciences found that, by every measure, active learning is more effective for every kind of student, in every discipline, versus the traditional lecture mode or the question-and-answer guided discussion method (Freeman et al. 2014). According to an *Inside Higher Ed* article, "Had [this] been a pharmaceutical study, traditional learning would be taken off the market" (2022).

So how are organizations already integrating experiential learning into their L&D repertoires? An article published by 360Learning lists "The 7 Best Experiential Learning Activities to Engage Employees" and includes roleplaying, simulations, and gamification. That might sound ho-hum, but it comes down to how you create the experiences and to what extent you use technology. What I found even more interesting was their list of ways to encourage experiential learning activities in your own organization:

1. Determine *why* you want to invest in experiential learning activities.

2. Make sure that your employees have easy access to all resources that support all phases of the experiential learning cycle.

3. Keep a strong feedback loop in place.

4. Encourage it as a part of company culture, not as a separate effort.

5. Experiential learning is a lot about self-discovery. Allow employees to connect their learnings to the world at large and not just limited to the workplace.

6. Experiential learning activities should not be the last stop of corporate learning. Instead, it should be a catalyst and a multistep process toward the finest workplace experience.

Give learners agency. Let them learn through experiments, making mistakes. Create learning experiences that are fun, and learners will eventually change their mindsets about learning—from boring and obligatory to exciting and engaging. Start by altering your own learning goals, objectives, and outcomes. Utilizing relevant teaching methods and modes will create better learning experiences that have a real impact on learners and their organizations (in the case of workplace learning).

To borrow from Daniel Pink's book *Drive*, through embracing experiential learning, we give learners autonomy, encourage them to gain a sense of purpose in structuring and owning their learning, and thus propel them toward mastery (2011). *Voila*!

CHAPTER 7

It's Transformational, My Dear Watson

People conduct countless transactions on a daily basis, whether we're buying groceries at the corner store, ordering books and cleaning supplies on Amazon, or paying utility bills. Likewise, businesses conduct transactions all day long; it is the process of purchasing and selling things. In addition, a transaction could be an interaction between two people, such as engaging in a conversation about politics. In all these examples, a transaction is essentially an exchange between two or more entities. You exchange X (like time or money) for Y (a product, service, or result).

All too often, learning looks and feels like a transaction. You take a course in exchange for a grade. You complete compliance and safety training to knock out a checklist of industry requirements. You zip through an online training module to meet mandates from human resources. Even within the curriculum or learning content itself, it can seem transactional or superficial. This is right. That is wrong. This is black. That is white. You earned enough points to pass. You may pass GO.

Aren't we missing something here?

Real, deep learning and transformation happen in the gray, where learners contemplate the unknown and possibilities; where they are free to think critically, consider options through analysis and synthesis, be creative and curious, and discover a variety of solutions to problems that might be off the grid. So, to spark higher-level learning, deep understanding and analysis, and a love of learning, we really need to create more relevant and applicable environments and experiences for learners. This is where meaningful transformation happens.

TRANSACTIONAL VERSUS TRANSFORMATIONAL LEARNING

Most teaching and training are transactional in nature, especially compliance training and process-oriented training. Most courses and their content focus on sharing knowledge, understanding key concepts, and basic skills building. Both parties—the instructors and the learners—have a role to play, and all too often it comes down to getting through a list of things people are supposed to learn in accordance with some prescribed criteria. And in many cases, we're trying to do this as quickly and conveniently as possible.

Back in 2020, the *Harvard Business Review* published an article entitled "The Transformer CLO," written by Abbie Lundberg and George Westerman. The authors interviewed twenty-one senior learning executives at companies such as

UBS and Accenture and found some interesting tidbits on how they're driving change. These change agents understand that corporate learning and development is no longer just about skills development; it must also include the development of *mindsets* (2020).

> Transformer CLOs are driving three principal types of change in their enterprises. They're transforming their organizations' learning goals, shifting the focus from the development of skills to the development of mindsets and capabilities that will help workers perform well now and adapt smoothly in the future. They're transforming their organizations' learning methods, making them more experiential and immediate, and atomizing content for delivery when and where it's needed. And they're transforming their organizations' learning departments, making them leaner, more agile, and more strategic (Lundberg and Westerman 2020, 1).

In addition, these companies embrace a growth mindset, which includes (1) enabling every employee to reach his or her fullest potential through professional development; and (2) baking this mindset into the overall culture. And the only way this can happen is if everyone has bought into the vision and is committed to transforming the learning experience (2020).

One notable example from the article showcased Accenture. Always comfortable with operating on the cutting edge, they utilize a variety of contemporary technologies and learning tools for professional development. That said, Rahul Varma, the senior managing director for talent at Accenture, understands that enabling cross-cultural and cross-functional teams to learn and work together *in person* is often the most engaging and effective. To balance the omnipresence of virtual and hybrid workplaces with the desire for people to feel connected, Accenture has created nearly one hundred globally dispersed "connected classrooms," whereby instructors as well as learners can be in different locations yet still have a personal and collaborative learning experience. "Thanks to videoconferencing and other interactive technologies, along with more collaborative approaches to learning, traditional geographic constraints no longer apply. Teams all over the world now coach one another and solve problems together," says Varma (2020).

I scoured multiple resources, including *Forbes* (Marr 2023) and *Fast Company* (Fennell 2024), to see what skills are in demand in the workplace today and for the next several years. Aside from hard tech skills, such as software development, coding, data analytics, and those related to emerging technologies, I continue to see the same topics at the top of the list. I'm starting to feel sorry for employers who just can't find people with (what appear to be) basic people, communications, and thinking skills for the modern-day workplace. Here are the skills that top employers' wish lists:

- Agility
- Communications
- Creativity
- Critical thinking
- Emotional intelligence and self-awareness
- People/interpersonal skills
- Problem solving
- Tech and data literacy

And just to seal the deal to confirm this is a global concern, check out this list from the World Economic Forum's Future Jobs Report (2023). Not only are these skills in demand *now*, but it is also predicted they will continue to grow in importance for the foreseeable future:

1. Creative thinking
2. Analytical thinking
3. Technological literacy
4. Curiosity and lifelong learning
5. Resilience, flexibility, and agility
6. Systems thinking
7. AI and big data
8. Motivation and self-awareness
9. Talent management
10. Service orientation and customer service

I suspect the challenge is that there's no one right way to become curious or creative or more self-aware. These things must be personally experienced to really stick. Cultivating these skills will also require learning leaders to consider new ways to teach such things such as agility. So many of these skills are transformative in and of themselves; therefore, the way in which they are taught must be experiential and transformative for the learners.

What exactly does transformational learning look like? Rather than giving you a definition, I'm going to share several examples of organizations that provide truly transformational environments, support systems, and growth opportunities for their students or employees. Even more fundamental than that, these organizations have created and continue to nurture learning cultures—not just in one department but throughout the entire organization. Let's touch on that first.

BUILDING A LEARNING CULTURE

A learning culture is when an organization prioritizes and supports continuous learning for its employees. Key words: prioritizes and continuous. Not only is this important for the long-term development of high performing individuals with in-demand skills, but it also alters people's mindsets and attitudes about learning. In such an environment, learning isn't approached as obligatory or something to knock off a to-do list. It isn't considered a one and done activity. Formal and informal learning occurs daily, and it never ends. *It never ends.* Learning cultures encourage experimenting and making mistakes. Learners are free to be curious and creative. If we want to encourage our people to be lifelong learners, having a strong learning culture is a great place to start.

One of the best definitions of learning culture I found was on TrainingIndustry.com, in an article written by Neil Bradley. A learning culture is: "A culture that supports an open mindset, an independent quest for knowledge, and shared learning directed toward the mission and goals of the organization" (2022).

While some organizations prioritize learning cultures, others find it too complex or time consuming to support. The most recent human capital trends survey from Deloitte found that less than half (only 43 percent) of surveyed participants reported that their organizations had a good learning culture, and only 11 percent said theirs was excellent (2019). Yikes! We've got a lot of work to do.

Building a learning culture requires complete buy-in from administrative and front-line employees all the way up the chain to C-level executives. Learning must be a priority organization-wide; not just perceived as a cost center that gets whacked during tough times. Employees must be given freedom to experiment, make mistakes, try new technologies, and challenge their peers as well as the status quo. All with a foundation of community and collaboration.

Developing a learning-centric culture should be fairly easy to manage because more freedom and agency is given to employees and learners. With some overarching goals and guidance from L&D experts, I think employees would be thrilled to manage their professional development paths. Yes, I understand some training is required, such as compliance and safety training, but many opportunities are available to empower employees to evolve in a way that aligns with their interests and strengths.

Ironically, one would think that by default, higher education institutions have learning cultures. While they may be delivering learning to students, the organizational culture in universities and colleges more often than not does not necessarily support or promote a learning culture for faculty and staff. The resources and funding set aside for professional development are scant, and the criteria for what you can spend said money on is pretty prescriptive. Therefore, faculty can rarely get support to learn something that's considered unconventional. Unfortunately, the emphasis, and thus resources, are carved out to support more research and publishing than developing those who are in the classroom teaching students. This is particularly true for top-tier research universities.

One university, however, does an exceptional job at nurturing a learning culture, and that is Arizona State University (ASU) under President Michael Crow's guidance. Crow's action-oriented personality and future-oriented mindset impact how he shapes ASU's education vision, including increased networking and community engagement to create a model of what he calls a "New American University," providing accessible education at scale and accelerating social change.

To achieve this, he led the development of a charter that includes a fresh mission and goals, as well as laying out plans for a new environment, a new community, new objectives, and nine design aspirations that are aligned with the overarching mission of the institution. The ASU community readily supports and lives by the charter, and they are *expected* to take action and demonstrate how they are living up to their commitment. The charter is a public statement on the ASU website (https://newamericanuniversity.asu.edu/about/asu-charter-mission-and-goals) and is meant to not only guide key constituents within the ASU ecosystem but also inspire other university leaders to think differently about their own mission and goals.

ASU has carved out an annual budget of $100 million for professional development, and Crow claims his faculty are unbelievably innovative. This is because ASU built a culture that lives and breathes the pursuit of innovation, and the faculty willingly embrace technology. The resources put behind professional development and support for faculty is impressive and envious. I liken this kind of culture to a petri dish for innovation, which in turn introduces students to new ways of learning, thinking, and creating.

A 2024 *Forbes* article entitled "Mind the (Skills) Gap" reports that one of the primary reasons employees ditch their jobs is because they don't have a clear path to professional opportunities and development. Giving employees guidance on what skills to acquire to grow in their profession along with the resources to obtain the training would make them (1) feel more valued, (2) feel more motivated, and (3) feel more committed to their employer. Making learning a priority in one's organizational culture sends a signal to employees that their upward mobility is important and their contributions are valued (Mosley 2024).

Learning cultures can also impact the bottom line of your organization, so the benefits go way beyond individual growth. Research conducted by Bersin & Associates about adaptive learning organizations found that companies with strong learning cultures are 92 percent more likely to innovate and 52 percent more productive compared to those without such cultures. As a leading HR analyst, Bersin applauds companies that dedicate the time and resources for experimentation and innovation, embracing the possibility of failure as a means of learning and valuing the contributions of all employees, irrespective of hierarchical levels (Bersin 2020).

Let's look at some leading institutions and organizations that (a) have strong learning cultures and (b) create environments that support transformational learning.

THE TRANSFORMERS

I've had the pleasure of speaking with exceptional leaders from some amazing organizations to gather examples for this book. I purposefully chose to include a variety of industries and sectors in the US, serving different levels of learners—from high school to higher education to professional development in the workplace. The driving force in these organizations often comes down to an individual or small team who are the visionaries and change agents. (Hats off to them!) Regardless of which industry or sector you are in, so many inspiring lessons and examples can be taken away from each of these transformers.

BLUE VALLEY SCHOOL DISTRICT
The Blue Valley School District in Kansas City, led by Corey Mohn, is a great example of driving transformational learning. Mohn is the president and executive director of the Center for Advanced Professional Studies (CAPS) Network, a program that serves local students from five public high schools in the district. These students come to the CAPS facility in Overland Park, Kansas, after an abridged day at school for several hours of discovery and hands-on learning to help them learn about business, explore career options, and to test the waters of a specific industry.

While it might sound a bit like a career center, the CAPS program is rather unique. The difference is that instead of focusing on vocational education or technical skills, CAPS empowers students to explore and engage in lots of self-discovery to give them more guidance regarding what they want to pursue after high school. The emphasis is on connecting students with the community and prioritizing experiential learning beyond traditional classroom boundaries. The CAPS program may start in a classroom, but it branches out widely to build relationships with local business partners that provide real-world opportunities for students to apply what they are learning in the classroom. For instance, a student might spark a relationship with a local startup or small business to explore their interests in entrepreneurship.

Such learning experiences might start with research and opportunity recognition, followed by the process of prototyping, and developing and testing a product—with mentorship all along the way. CAPS's commitment to pushing boundaries and fostering a mindset of experimentation and self-discovery really resonates with students and creates stellar outcomes. With its focus beyond just project outcomes and stressing the importance of adaptive, flexible workplace skills rather than technicalities, leaders like Mohn are creating both a transformative environment and transformative experiences for students.

The transformational learning begins when students do an exercise with the purpose compass because the key to their success in CAPS is matching the student's curiosity and strengths with real-time, authentic opportunities. Students are tasked with finding what sits at the intersection of what they love to do, what their strengths and skills are, and what problem or need exists in the world. It's a thought-provoking exercise that indeed helps identify one's true north.

Mohn and his students wish activities like this were baked into the public school curriculum, but again, it's difficult to get educators to think differently and try something new. In school, students are sort of programmed to operate with prescribed steps and processes, i.e., what to do, how to do it, and what the right and wrong answers are. Read this. Do this. Take this test. Here's your score. What Mohn is offering the students is the opportunity to manage projects with lots of ambiguity, which is much more representative of real life. CAPS learners are comfortable with problem solving, taking initiative, asking questions, and wandering through the halls of ambiguity. Now *this* is how to prepare young people for the real world.

When I asked Mohn about the learning culture that has been cultivated at CAPS, he said it comes down to two words: collegial and community. Collegial, meaning that students and mentors and instructors are on an even playing field. Students have agency. They are encouraged to take the lead and work side-by-side with their mentors. Hierarchy doesn't exist here, which changes up the entire power structure the students are used to elsewhere. Community refers to the strong relationships that are formed at CAPS with internal and external key constituents. CAPS has created a culture akin to an extended family more than a career center, and that kind of supportive, nurturing environment is what enables students to spread their wings.

CUYAHOGA COMMUNITY COLLEGE
I honestly never knew much about two-year colleges until I had the privilege of speaking with Dr. Michael Baston, president of Cuyahoga Community College (Tri-C) in Cleveland, Ohio. He totally opened my eyes to the differences in how two- and four-year institutions operate, and how much more agile community colleges can be since (1) faculty aren't handcuffed with things like tenure or publishing requirements, and (2) they serve a different market.

To say I am super impressed with the agility and responsiveness happening at Tri-C would be an understatement. As the captain steering the ship at Tri-C since 2022, Dr. Baston said that much of the change happening there is in direct response to the pandemic, but the transformation is also quite deliberate under his leadership. He is extremely grounded in Tri-Cs mission, which is economic mobility.

"We use education as the vehicle for that specific mission. Our mission is to say that regardless of what zip code you live in, and regardless of whatever circumstances you have had in your life, we are going to help you move forward. Our mission is to make sure you are a viable citizen, that you get to participate in the same prosperity that everyone else in our country gets to participate in."

This speaks volumes to the learners who enroll at Tri-C. They are there to learn, provide for their families, earn promotions and better career opportunities, and more. Their goals and expectations are quite different from many traditional college students who might be more interested in frat parties and football games. Dr. Baston is so in tune with his population. Their goals light the fire in his belly to offer the most cutting-edge, relevant learning experience possible at Tri-C.

"Many of [the students] are going part-time because they're working full-time and they're pulling together a strategy to move themselves forward. So, we have to be responsive to their needs. We have to make sure we can provide them in-demand credentials that move them economically forward, relatively quickly. And so it is incumbent upon us to think differently. We can't rely on the older ways of managing and moving forward. We think deeply about that agility, that flexibility."

What is fascinating to me is that a community college can be so much more responsive and move much faster than the vast majority of four-year institutions. This kind of fast-paced change could really give community colleges a competitive advantage over four-year institutions, especially when high school students and their families are looking for a good value for their money.

What else sets Tri-C apart?

Right off the bat, Dr. Baston mentioned the importance of investing in the professional development of his staff. One of the things Baston has done to create a learning culture at Tri-C is build out a Dean's Academy to help faculty, deans, directors, and department heads understand the labor market, as well as the pipeline for student job placements. He recognizes that in order to achieve certain outcomes (i.e., job placement for graduates), you have to educate the people who are responsible for helping to produce those outcomes. "As much as we want to teach, we have to actually *know*, because you can't give what you don't know," says Baston.

In addition, Tri-C offers resources through their Center for the Future of Work to staff right alongside the students. This includes externships so staff can gain relevant professional experience beyond the walls of academia. Tri-C also provides certifications for all sorts of programs to support the professional growth of his team. It sounds like it is a bit infectious versus obligatory for staffers. They actually show up and are hungry to learn more, more, more.

One of my biggest complaints is that higher education doesn't pay enough attention to what is going on beyond their silos and fiefdoms on campus. They are often out of touch with the demands in the workplace and therefore don't even know if what they're teaching is of economic value to their students. Like Corey Mohn's CAPS program, Baston is adamant about engaging with local businesses and communities. These external partners are Tri-C's ears and eyes to the work world. These alliances and conversations inform Tri-C what they should be doing to support their student's success. This is the missing piece at so many institutions! Props to you, Dr. Baston, for understanding how important this is for students.

He also shared, "There was a time when you learned for a specific purpose, to do a specific task or be on a specific track. Well, that's not how it works today. Educational institutions are recognizing that we can't just offer what we *think* people want, or we *think* people should know, or we *think* people should receive. We have to respond to the interests, concerns, and ways in which people want to live and work." That's agility, folks.

He tied up the conversation with a nice big bow telling me what he believes are the five critical things—five simple but very action-oriented things—necessary to build the framework of a transformative organization. Here they are:

1. Study: start with the facts of your contacts.
2. Speak: stand by what you believe in.
3. See: understand the needs of those you serve.
4. Seek: understand who cares about what you care about.
5. Serve: do what you can until you can do more.

Transformational learning and strong learning cultures begin with the conviction of great leaders like Dr. Baston. And Tri-C is proof that you don't need a big endowment or a big brand name to be an agile institution that delivers value for students.

MINERVA UNIVERSITY

I see countless universities touting how innovative they are in each issue of *The Chronicle of Higher Education* and each school's respective website, but Minerva University is one of the few institutions that walk the walk and execute innovative initiatives on so many levels with measurable impact. They are already *way* outside the box. Minerva has carved out their own path that is so unlike most higher education institutions. I love, love, love the type of educational experiences they provide for their students. They put innovation and transformational learning at the center of their mission. They truly develop problem solvers and analytical thinkers in their degree programs, which goes hand in hand with fostering an entrepreneurial mindset.

I had the most electric conversation with Dr. Dollie Davis, dean of faculty at Minerva University, several months ago. She elaborated on what makes Minerva so special and stand out as a leader in transformational learning.

"Everything we do at Minerva is intentional. The university was built with a focus on lifelong learning and follows learning principles from cognitive science. We focus on teaching critical thinking and communication skills before we teach hard skills. That way, students are set up to be able to think deeply and analyze the topics we teach them in their more focused classes like finance or linear algebra. All classes are flipped, where students prepare for class before it happens and then each class is fully active with absolutely no lecturing and packed with several interactive discussions and activities. We assess student's application of their critical thinking skills and their knowledge of the class concepts in and out of the classroom so that students can work with regular feedback in order to improve their application of these skills. Finally, Minerva students travel all over the globe over their four years and, as such, complete immersive, applied projects in different cities which they tie back into their coursework, thereby strengthening their skills as well as their cultural dexterity."

Minerva University is definitely not your typical university. While they might not be able to offer frat life or football games, the world is your campus. The life lessons learned through travel and learning by doing are directly applicable to what students are studying and the careers for which they are preparing. In my humble opinion, this type of education is worth every penny (versus other degree-granting programs) and delivers on their promise to develop globally aware problem solvers with hungry souls and inquisitive minds. Precisely what companies are looking for.

MARRIOTT INTERNATIONAL

Mark Boccia, EdD, is a global learning and development executive with vast experience at leading companies such as Amazon, Royal Caribbean, and Marriott International. He shared some amazing stories with me about how he's led transformational learning programs throughout his career.

One really creative project he developed and led was something called "How My Hotel Works" at Marriott International. Here's Mark's story:

"'How My Hotel Works' was an initiative to give non-facilities managers and non-engineers the eyes and ears and senses to notice things like a leaky faucet, a crack in the sidewalk, or to identify the presence of mold. Most of the time people aren't cognizant of these things, so the objective of the project was to pinpoint problems early and address them before they escalate to avoid unnecessary spending. At the time, virtual reality was coming into the fore. It was very early on, but I designed a whole immersive learning series for 'How My Hotel Works.' We did a creative spin with actors that could put a comedic routine in a short skit. It allowed for informational, educational, and entertainment factors. For each of the buildings that participated, we gave them a VR headset to create issue spotting activities. People would walk around the property identifying problems and estimating how much it would cost to fix it early versus what it would cost if you let go for a year. We added the extra business and math component to make it real. The operations leaders and the engineering team were partnered up with the maintenance guys to learn together and fix issues together. And it saved Marriott loads of money."

Boccia also believes that learning needs to be a brand and treated as a brand. "What's the brand message? What are your brand pillars? What do you stand for? Your learning brand has to be established and communicated, and it needs to be managed like a brand manager would. Of course you have to have solid content and have all the other tick boxes of being effective, a good use of time and learning measures, but a static class on its own doesn't sell, and it doesn't have much impact. But there's no shelf life on a really great experience. If you have a really good learning experience, it tugs on emotion. It provides you with something memorable. I know for a fact I can pull from memorable experiences from two decades ago that still stick and help shape and morph how I think, how I act, and so forth."

SO WHAT? NOW WHAT?

Back in 2010, Josh Bersin published a report entitled, "High-Impact Learning Culture: A New Era in Corporate Learning & Development" (2010). Through his research, he discovered how impactful a strong learning culture can be. For example, high-performing organizations are three times more likely to have a strong learning culture, and the strength of a learning culture is directly, and positively, correlated to organizational performance. He noted, "The single biggest driver of business impact is the strength of an organization's learning culture" (Bradley 2022).

Baking in components such as building trust, empowering employees, and formalizing learning as a process are key to establishing a learning culture. And in turn, business outcomes such as learning agility, innovation, productivity, and customer satisfaction catapult to new heights. Notice the inputs and outputs of the transformer organizations mentioned earlier. The impact is a game changer at all levels. That's why developing and nurturing the right environment driven by future-forward leaders can set you and your constituents apart from the competition. This is the foundation for creating transformational learning experiences for those you serve.

As we begin transitioning to be more visionary, out-of-the-box thinkers, this will eventually become the norm at education institutions and organizations alike. Learners will come to expect transformational learning to be value-add performers and to be prepared for whatever this world slings at them.

I look at it this way: Remember at the turn of the last century how the big buzz was "e-" everything? E-mail. E-commerce. E-learning. E-book. E-business. E-cigarettes. Over time, it becomes less necessary to use that designation in many instances because the digital version of things has become more of the norm than an anomaly. For example, almost 20 percent of commerce is conducted online these days. How much more e-mail do you read versus snail mail? Isn't just about every business an e-business by default with websites and the ability to buy, sell, and do things online?

So keep this "e-" example in mind and understand that initially it takes time for people to adapt to new ways of doing or behaving or learning. You may experience some resistance and hiccups and frustration. But once nouveau things, systems, and ways of being become more omnipresent and we understand them, we will begin to operate and learn on a higher level. We need to go through our own transformation to in turn provide more transformational learning opportunities for our students and employees. I equate this to the caterpillar that's in its chrysalis morphing into something completely new and amazing.

CHAPTER 8

Ready or Not, Here It Comes

EMERGING TECHNOLOGIES

Do you remember back in the mid-1990s when the internet was creeping into our lives? So much was unknown. So much misinformation, and plenty of caution, fear, disbelief, and skepticism. What a ride it has been since then! But here we are, thirty years later. Could you even imagine life without the internet and email? Think back to how you adopted this new technology. Did you dive in and get your own personal computer? Did you buy a modem and sign up for dial-up service? Do you remember the early entrants to the market? Gateway. Dell. America Online. Yahoo. Netscape. And then… Apple and Microsoft. We experimented with the hardware and software. Things weren't perfect in the beginning, but the user experience was evolving at warp speed.

The introduction of anything new that drives significant change is often met with resistance from the general public. This is a normal human reaction. When the change is sparked by technological innovation, it seems the walls of resistance are exponentially higher. Sadly, with all the benefits technology offers, there can be negative consequences and those who exploit said technologies for the wrong reasons (e.g., spreading terrorism, money laundering, fake news, and the list goes on).

Regardless, my firm belief is that the benefits of technology far outweigh the drawbacks. And whether we like it or not, technological advancements pose new possibilities for the ways we live, communicate, socialize, work, play, and learn. This doesn't need to be a scary proposition. Our relationship with technology is similar to tax law: We can't possibly understand it all, but the more we know, the more power we have in our own hands.

After scouring multiple sources, including recent reports such as Educause Horizon Report: Teaching and Learning Edition (2024) and the EY Emerging Tech at Work survey (Alam and Barrington 2023), it is clear that a few technology trends are having—and will continue to have—the most impact on adult education and workplace learning. These include:

- Artificial intelligence
- Extended reality
- Big data
- Predictive analytics

Some reports and predictions, including "The 11 Game-Changing L&D Trends of 2024" from MDA Training, an experiential learning consulting firm, also indicate that personalized learning and microlearning are tech trends in the industry (2024). But these are the *result* of using certain technologies. I wouldn't consider them technologies. Emerging technologies *enable* learners to have more personalized or customized learning experiences, and microlearning refers to *how* learners access and consume learning. That said, it is important to keep these learning trends in mind.

Since 2018, LinkedIn has annually produced rather robust Workplace Learning Reports. One of the most recent reports from 2024 surveyed over 1,600 L&D and HR professionals and contains some reaffirming—and in some cases eye-popping—data (2024). Yes, AI has taken center stage in the conversation as it has for essentially every department in organizations, but aside from figuring out how to utilize AI-related tools on the job, L&D leaders are charged with learning how to use AI tools for professional development purposes—in a meaningful, value-add way. This is equally daunting and exciting. Okay, AI aside, what's top of mind for companies?

Ninety-one percent of the L&D professionals who were surveyed for this report noted that soft skills are increasingly important. Why do I mention this here? Because *what* needs to be taught dictates which emerging technologies should be utilized. For example, if the number one skill in demand in the workplace was accounting, I don't think extended reality (XR) would be the best option to enhance the learner experience. XR adds value when learners are dealing with topics that have more than one right best answer or there are many ways to solve something. Negotiating is a good example. On the other hand, a topic like accounting is based on many rules. Therefore, the calculations and outcomes are rather black and white. In this case, AI might be a better solution to guide learners in understanding predominantly predictable answers.

Let's focus on the three emerging technologies that are predicted to have the greatest impact on learning—much like the introduction of the internet over thirty years ago.

ARTIFICIAL INTELLIGENCE
One way we can immediately drive change is leveraging artificial intelligence in study or work routines. AI has gained a problematic reputation within learning circles, and with cause. Educators and trainers worry that the use of AI could diminish a significant portion of human interaction in the learning process, resulting in a loss of social skills, and could make learners and facilitators vulnerable to privacy and security breaches. Yet considered another way, AI becomes a huge "teaching moment" for facilitators to demonstrate comfort with disruption and change, illustrate analytical thinking that helps humans separate the grain from the chaff, and practice how the scale of AI can be balanced with the rigor of human(e) considerations.

Within the world of education and training, many use cases illustrate where AI is most useful and impactful: creating content, generating assessment questions, adaptive learning, and just-in-time guidance. In addition to these, we are seeing AI used in virtual role-playing scenarios with AI-generated avatars and real-time support using chatbots. What are the real benefits to learners, and what does it mean for learning leaders?

CHATBOTS

Chatbots have been around for a while, but with the onset of powerful AI tools such as ChatGPT from OpenAI, learners are able to get answers and guidance when they need it. This is similar to Google in that we have answers at our fingertips, but AI-powered chatbots can be more specific, leading to a more customized learning experience.

A cool example of this can be found on the leading language learning site Duolingo. A few years ago, Duolingo introduced a new product called Duolingo Max, which is supported by GPT-4. Two of their new features are called Explain My Answer and Roleplay. Explain My Answer enables learners to get immediate feedback on a lesson or exercise that they might be having trouble with. What happens if you make the same mistake over and over again but don't know why and just need a little extra guidance or explanation? Utilizing GPT-4, Duolingo is able to automatically provide an explanation, further clarification, and additional examples to help learners understand where they went wrong and how to correct themselves (2023).

Here's another example. Udacity is an online learning company that leverages massive open online courses (MOOCs) to teach technology and business topics. They utilize Chat GPT-4 as an "intelligent virtual tutor" to help their students work through complex technical problems when they don't have access to instructors. The chatbot is particularly useful for learners who might not be native English speakers because Chat GPT-4 can rather quickly translate content and technical jargon into other languages (Marr 2023). Just think how difficult this is to do under normal circumstances.

ADAPTIVE LEARNING

Most courses and modules are developed to take people through learning in the same order and essentially at the same pace. This format doesn't take into consideration that some people might already know some of the content but are required to complete it anyhow. Or someone might be starting off with no prior experience or information and perhaps needs extra support and guidance.

The two categories for adaptive learning tools are: simple and complex. Simple adaptive tools are more linear in nature when tracking a learner's progress. We see this in some standardized tests where if you get an answer correct, you are led in one direction to the next question. If you didn't answer the question correctly, you are led in a different direction to a different question that perhaps isn't as difficult. While this does accommodate learners to an extent, it isn't entirely adaptive because the steps are predefined.

On the other hand, complex adaptive tools use additional data sources to determine next steps. In this case, AI takes into consideration other learner data in addition to previous answers, including the number of interactions or complex conditions, then pairs this information with logical rules that take the learner on a more personalized path (Baraishuk 2023).

Adaptive learning allows for a more customized learning experience and a streamlined process. According to an article by Mary K. Pratt about the use cases for adaptive AI, she notes:

> Adaptive AI is powered by various techniques, including ML [machine learning], reinforcement learning, neural

networks, agent-based modeling and evolutionary algorithms. The fact that it's a mix, or composite, of different AI technologies puts adaptive AI in the broader category of composite AI. This combination of technologies enables adaptive AI to change its own code in response to changing circumstances and its experiences over time. As such, it can improve its own performance and accuracy as it operates (Pratt 2023).

AI algorithms pick up how the learner learns, where they might be struggling, and then adapt questions, exercises, or activities to help them stay on track. And then tools like reinforcement learning mimic the trial-and-error learning process that humans are used to. For example, once we set our learning goals, any learner actions that are in alignment with those goals are reinforced or rewarded; those that stray from the goals are either ignored or realigned to the proper path. I don't think it's necessary to understand how the algorithms work—it's complex—but it's important for us to know how adaptive learning can improve the experience and outcomes for learners while also enabling us to be more attuned to their individual journeys.

AI-POWERED AVATARS

We have begun experimenting with AI-powered avatars on the Edstutia campus in VR. This is a great example of how emerging technologies can meld to create an even better learning experience. Here's how it works:

Avatars can now be programmed to take on identities, personas, priorities, and even a particular expertise or language. Imagine being able to do a roleplaying exercise with such an avatar to practice certain skills, such as conflict resolution or preparing for an interview. The experience is significantly better than going through a scripted or canned conversation because of the free flow of dialogue and because no two conversations are alike. You can ask the avatar anything you want within the scope of the topic and spark up a robust, realistic conversation. Avatars can also express emotion, such as anger or frustration, and exemplify that through body language, so the interaction is more authentic than you would expect.

Here's a specific example: We can program an avatar to take on the role of an HR executive who has a professional persona and demeanor as well as criteria for identifying the right candidate for a specific role. We can tell the avatar what key words or answers to look for. We can program what the objectives of the interaction are and what the ultimate outcome should be. On top of that, we now have the ability to include assessment tools, such as rubrics, whereby AI can calculate how well the roleplay went and spit out a report telling the human participant what went well as well as what needs improvement.

I wouldn't perceive this as if AI and avatars are going to steal our jobs. AI can make our lives easier by reducing the time spent on time-consuming, mundane tasks like grading, which then frees up more of our time for personal interaction. What is also amazing is the accuracy of the AI-generated assessments, so that should give you peace of mind.

EXTENDED REALITY (XR)

Back in 2018, I put on a VR headset for the first time. I was still working in higher education, and we had a local VR developer, The Glimpse Group, come to campus to do a demo for business school faculty. I was blown away. As a lifelong learner in search of new ways to engage and inspire learners, I was immediately convinced this technology would change learning forever. And I still feel that way today.

Before we move on any further, I think it's important to clarify what extended reality (XR) is. XR is an umbrella term that includes virtual reality (VR), augmented reality (AR), and mixed reality (MR). These are all types of immersive technologies, which essentially lie at the intersection of the physical world and a digital or simulated world.

Augmented Reality	Virtual Reality	Mixed Reality
Think of this as a filter overlapping something in the real world that provides additional information in different media—audio, video, data, etc.	True immersions in VR include wearing a VR headset that transports you to a different place, a new dimension. The outside—or real—world can be completely blocked out. In immersive spaces and environments, you feel a real sense of presence somewhere else with others who might physically be halfway around the world.	This is a combination of AR and VR, whereby you can produce digital assets and media as if you were in VR, but you can still see your true surroundings.
Examples: Hovering over a painting at a museum with an AR app on your smartphone to watch a period video of the artist in their art studio, or sharing a song or photo that inspired their work.	Examples: Whether it is playing collaborative games, visiting historical ruins or going on a journey inside the human body, VR encapsulates you to personally experience things firsthand.	Examples: Placing computer-generated furniture in your home, virtual field trips with Google Expeditions, or virtual makeup applications are common examples.

Since my first foray into XR, the technology has evolved exponentially, from devices to platforms to content to functionality. With the proliferation of more devices (some with a decreasing price tag), access to more content and platform providers, the improvement of software that makes avatars and immersive experiences more life-like, and increased knowledge of the value of using XR, we are seeing year-over-year growth. As a matter of fact, the XR market size is expected to grow to $111.5 billion by 2028. North America and Europe, not surprisingly, are at the forefront with respect to developing and using XR (Markets and Markets 2024). Personal experience indicates the world is still looking to the United States as the leader, not only in usage but the development of a growing ecosystem. Another source, Mordor Intelligence, estimates the VR market size will triple in size from 2024 to $187.4 billion by 2030 (2024). Any way you slice it, this is astronomical growth that can't be ignored.

Essentially every industry will be impacted by the growing presence of XR—from education and professional development to manufacturing, retail, healthcare and more—with different use cases including medical procedures, manufacturing operations, inventory management, automotive design, safety and compliance training, and conceptual design. Here are some examples of how XR is specifically reshaping the education and training landscape.

METAVERSITIES
Steve Grubbs, the CEO of VictoryXR, is a global leader in the education metaverse. VictoryXR specializes in building custom 3D replications of university campuses, also referred

to as digital twins. Creating a virtual version of a campus allows anyone access to that campus from anywhere in the world without the typical expenses of attending a university in person, e.g., transportation expenses and cost-of-living expenses near campus. All students can now access the same buildings, rooms, and facilities, no matter where they are located. Without such physical barriers, this opens the playing field, making access to education easier for a wider audience.

Not only can VictoryXR create digital twins and content for post-secondary institutions, but they also serve K–12, homeschoolers, and corporate markets. To date, they have partnered with over fifty higher education institutions to create digital campuses, including campus grounds, building interiors and exteriors, sports venues, and even dorms. One of the most notable examples of a metaversity is Morehouse College in Atlanta, Georgia. It takes a visionary leader like Muhsinah Morris, the metaversity director, to pull this off. By being an early adopter, Morehouse College is paving the way for other universities to learn the ropes and get on board to deliver immersive, engaging learning experiences for their students. Not only does this initiative give Morehouse College a competitive advantage, but all of the students learning in and about immersive tech will also certainly stand out among their peers when it comes time for job interviews (Cairns 2023).

XR IN THE WORKPLACE

Accenture, always known for being an early adopter, developed their own virtual space called "The Nth Floor" as we were crawling out of the pandemic. It is a space where

Accenture employees can meet, collaborate, and learn—no matter where they are located. This proved to be a great option for continued socialization, collaboration, and productivity after all the social distancing during COVID. That said, many Accenture employees, by nature of their consulting business, work remotely or at client sites, so this new space is a welcomed way to build team cohesion. In addition to The Nth Floor, Accenture has also created digital twins (similar to metaversities) of some of its physical offices around the world. To support these efforts, Julie Sweet, Accenture CEO, invested in sixty thousand Meta Quest headsets back in 2021 specifically for training and onboarding purposes (Fink 2021).

Another way Accenture leverages VR is for onboarding new hires, which they refer to as "new joiners." Many of these experiences are developed by Olly Jeffers, global onboarding innovation lead, and his team. While some employees are enthusiastic about immersing themselves using a VR headset, others prefer a 2D version of the experience. Either way, the point is that Accenture employees who are scattered around the globe can meet, work, learn, collaborate, and socialize in a new dimension. Not only is learning sticky, but so are the teams (HRD Connect 2023).

To date, Accenture has onboarded more than 150,000 new joiners in their metaverse. Surveys indicate that 94 percent of new employees that went through the virtual onboarding were in favor of the virtual format. In addition, they have hosted hundreds of virtual gatherings, even at the C-level (HRD Connect 2023).

What about VR training? What's the impact? An Accenture report entitled "Meeting the New Reality: Immersive Learning," shared that, when referring to traditional training courses, "learners forget 70 percent of the content within twenty-four hours and nearly 90 percent in a month." Interestingly, a related study found immersive VR instruction offered a path to achieve 33 percent higher learning retention when compared to video (2021).

Speed to learning, efficiencies of scale, learner engagement, and retention all see significant spikes when organizations offer VR-enhanced training. For Accenture and many other companies, this is a worthwhile investment, especially considering the longer-term benefits.

BIG DATA

When we speak of big data, we are not only referring to the massive amounts of data we are able to collect in our data-driven world, but also the technologies and techniques used to process, store, and manipulate said data at granular levels (WEKA 2022). Learning professionals who have operated without such information for years might not immediately see the value and benefits of these technologies, but all of this information helps us to become better teachers/trainers and improve the learning experience for our learners. It's a win-win but certainly requires some adapting and adopting on our part.

How does this impact the learning industry? Today, we have the ability to gather endless amounts of data about our learners that in turn can help us understand whether we are achieving our learning objectives, where learners might be struggling, and how we can improve the individual learning experience through more personalization—in addition to many other things. Learner outcomes become much clearer when we are able to collect learner data throughout a course or program. As it stands today, we all too often collect superficial learner data such as quiz or test scores *at the end* of a course or program, which is too late to make iterative improvements during the course. That is a lost opportunity.

Thankfully, learning management systems (LMS) are beginning to expand their capabilities by capturing and processing ever more data about learners. It isn't really about test scores anymore. Not only can we track learner engagement, progress, understanding, and practical application, but algorithms can analyze, synthesize, and report meaningful learner data for a much more comprehensive picture of each learner's progress. And much like the AI example above—because these calculations are done *for* us—it frees up our time to be more engaged with learners. This fundamentally changes the role of teachers and trainers.

An article entitled "How to Enhance Your LMS with Big Data and Learning Analytics" showcased some of the types of big data used in learning management systems, including which metrics can be captured and what the benefits are (Terehin 2023). See a summary in the following table. I find this useful to understand the vast benefits of big data to the learners, not just us learning leaders.

Completion rates	The data shows if your employees or students are actually completing the course and how long it takes them to finish up each task or module. It also gives you a good indication of the learning program's effectiveness. If most of the learners are unable to complete the course, it's a sure sign to reevaluate your learning strategy.
Performers and progress of your learners	Using big data for learning management systems brings insight into learning behaviors, experience, and proficiency.
Assessment scores	The percentage of passing grades gives you the power to identify online learners' strengths and weaknesses, which you use to personalize learning paths.
Surveys	This is a direct form of feedback, where you can find out honest opinions and recommendations.
Peer-based feedback	Social media groups, forums, online group collaboration projects, and learner-generated online content are the sources of peer-based feedback. With their help, you can see how online learners respond in social environments.

Many of these metrics are fundamental measurements that educators typically capture, of which I'm not a big fan. But when used in a contemporary way with relevant and plentiful data, the metrics are more useful. I am, however, a big fan of using different metrics that are more action oriented, and these are also enhanced with the presence of big data. Now, what do we do with all this data? That's where predictive analytics enters the picture.

PREDICTIVE ANALYTICS
Predictive analytics is simply using large amounts of historical data to predict future outcomes or events and is deeply connected with big data (WEKA 2022).

Predictive analytics can have a significant impact in essentially any industry, e.g., by predicting buying behavior, predicting technology trends, or identifying potential flaws in systems or processes. With respect to learning, predictive analytics empowers learning professionals to deliver better experiences and outcomes to their learners because the activities and processes can be personalized on an individual level.

An article hot off the press from eLearning Industry entitled "From Data To Action: Predicting and Enhancing Learner Success" highlights several benefits of leveraging predictive analytics (Kanaki 2025). In this case, the article is looking specifically at the workplace, but the findings are equally applicable in higher education. What are the benefits?

1. The ability to create tailored learning experiences.
2. The ability to design more poignant courses and exercises.
3. The ability to identify and assist learners who might be falling behind or struggling with specific concepts—earlier rather than later.
4. Increased learner engagement and decreased turnover.

Data-driven decision making will lead to improved results all around. We no longer have to guess, surmise, deduce, or make conclusions based off superficial data. We can iterate along the way instead of finding out useful information at the end of a session with surveys or evaluations. This is a game changer that feeds continuous improvement and can truly impact the bottom line of an organization.

TRENDS TO WATCH

The aforementioned technologies are four of the primary ones that will be the big drivers of change in education and professional development. But we also need to keep our eyes on other trending tech developments. They are already present today, but their impact specifically on learning will continue to make headway in the coming years. From Yogini's and my experience in adult learning, here are our top four:

TREND	IMPLICATIONS FOR LEARNERS
Cloud Computing	Accessing information and digital tools on any device from a secure server. Supports virtual collaboration at scale.
Gamification	Interactive games promote collaboration and competition, which increase learner engagement and motivation.
Internet of Things	Linking various digital devices supports collaboration and accessibility.
Robotics	Can be used as real-time tutors and used to understand complex topics to strengthen critical thinking and problem-solving skills.

FROM THE EXPERTS

I spoke with several tech and EdTech experts to get their personal insights on where technology is heading and how it will impact learning in the near future. I can't help but think of Wayne Gretzky's famous quote: "I skate to where the puck is going to be, not where it has been." So, where emerging technology *is headed* is what we should really be thinking about.

Lyron Bentovim
President and CEO
The Glimpse Group

Bentovim agrees that the biggest opportunity before us is the convergence of AI and XR, for both devices and software. We have already seen technologies that enable instructors to bring the world into the classroom—which is great!—but over the next twenty years, we're going to see more use cases of immersive technologies bringing the classroom into the world.

The current immersive tech cycle combines immersive technologies (VR/AR/MR) with AI and blockchain technologies to move society from the digital age to a fully immersive world. AI will allow us to effectively create new immersive 3D worlds that will—in addition to being future destinations for entertainment, v-commerce, travel, and future offices—allow learners to go out and actively experience historical eras (think ancient Greece or the Civil War in America).

Within the context of workplace learning, these technologies will converge to create unlimited science labs and job simulation platforms, thereby enabling students to actively learn about the past while developing skills that will build their future. These AI worlds and simulations will be mostly brought to life by AI-driven nonplayer characters (NPCs) that will be assigned the knowledge and personality to play each needed role.

Spatial computing will allow these worlds and simulations to run 24-7 in the cloud, streaming to more streamlined glasses that will need no processing power since the compute will happen in the cloud. The glasses will be easy to wear for longer periods of time and will have minimal power source needs, eventually evolving into contact lenses.

Over time, AI-powered NPCs will also become a part of the teaching process itself, serving as personal tutors and guides that can adapt to each student's personality, learning styles, and preferences, as well as challenges.

Matt Donovan
Chief Learning and Innovation Officer
GP Strategies Corporation

In addition to being a huge proponent of AI, Donovan believes several other technologies related to Web3.0 will have a major impact on how we learn. He also indicated which are still emerging and which are already here. That's an important differentiator because some of us might not even know what's happening under our noses, and as leaders in our field we need to be well informed and prepared. Read: *way* more than AI is disrupting our world.

EXISTING TECHNOLOGIES

Blockchain
The blockchain allows you to have a single transparent data truth, i.e., a single point of truth around the skills, capabilities, and learning journey for a learner. This ties to one's digital identity and enables a trusted, secure source. It also enables micro-transactions, which means smaller pieces of content can be purchased in smaller increments.

Generative AI
This is using big data and big data tools to capture massive datasets for the individual user, e.g., the evolution of personalized learning.

Semantic search
This allows for more meaningful search, providing deeper, more accessible results. This can have a significant impact around performance support systems. We are already seeing this as a byproduct of blending traditional search engines with generative AI.

EMERGING TECHNOLOGIES

> **Decentralized and distributed addressing system (a.k.a. IPFS)**
> This democratizes the creation of, access to, and sharing of individually generated content. Instead of having to go through domains, individual authors, creators, and educators can share information directly with learners or consumers. This could have the impact of opening up higher education offerings. For example, you could have a degree built from content across multiple universities, industry groups, companies, and individuals.
>
> **Unique digital, trusted identity**
> Imagine getting your digital identity at birth like your SSN. Your learning information would be attached to this digital identity and offers the individual more control and ownership over their digital identity and the associated data. You would no longer need centralized identity brokers; you share and rescind directly with organizations as you need.
>
> **Complete connectivity**
> This is about the interoperability of web applications, information, and experience.

Steve Grubbs
CEO
VictoryXR

Grubbs predicts that an amalgamation of technologies will be driving change in the world of learning. For example, he sees the 3D spatial/virtual reality world combining with AI, particularly in the form of conversational avatars and nonplayer characters (NPCs). This intersection leads to a more natural interaction between those seeking knowledge (learners) and the entities delivering knowledge (teachers, trainers, tutors) because the AI interface won't be just a 2D experience with lots of typing but rather in 3D form as interactive avatars.

Now, the avatars would need to be programmed with specific knowledge about a specific topic so they are able to share knowledge, answer questions, and troubleshoot with learners. He also envisions making this available to larger populations through a browser (such as Chrome) versus only through a VR headset. The evolution of the VR headset is also going to contribute to the larger adoption of 3D spatial AI. He predicts that Ray-Ban's Meta Smart Glasses will become increasingly powerful and soon replace the bulky headsets on the market today. Until the time when we are all injected with AI chips, a device or an interface is still necessary to access information.

Nathaly Tschanz
Professor of Immersive Technologies
Director of the Immersive Realities Center
Lucerne University of Applied Sciences and Arts

Tschanz's crystal ball predicts that gaming will continue to trend upward along with immersive tech and AI. The real value comes when all these technologies can work together. That will be both a huge disruption and mind-blowing potential wrapped up in one.

Since Tschanz tends to work with undergraduate students at Lucerne University, she's noticed specific things about how this younger generation prefers to live, learn, and socialize. "Immersive technologies [resonate with] the younger generations because they grew up in a completely different way. They spend a lot of time in digital worlds; they play a lot of games. They expect gamification from learning. They want learning to be fun." As an educator, she understands that we can't teach these learners in an old-fashioned way because they simply won't respond to it. She gets it but wants to spread the word to other educators that it is imperative we all shift to accommodate younger generations.

Because these new generations are highly visual, you have to show them—rather than explain with words—so that they understand it, because they're very used to visual representation. So whether we utilize augmented reality, virtual reality, or serious games, the learning experience has to be immersive. It has to address various senses and have a high level of gamification baked into it.

Another trend Tschanz sees value in is individualized learning. "I think this is getting more important because the new generations are no longer interested in mass products. They want to be addressed where they are at the moment, and they want to have targeted learning objectives, targeted on personal interests."

Tyler Gates
General Manager of Brightline Interactive
Chief Futurist of The Glimpse Group

Gates is bullish on XR for many reasons, but he reminded me that we have barely scratched the surface of what's possible with spatial computing. "The future of XR is streaming to the XR device. And without a spatial computing source, we can't fully realize the true potential of XR devices." Compare this to renting physical VHS tapes from Blockbuster with streaming movies on demand with Netflix. The experience is much more valuable and personal. He also likens XR devices as portals that lead us to a new format of learning and understanding one another. They are also mechanisms for the delivery of spatial computing, which is essentially a pipeline to sharing information.

He also sees headsets and other devices becoming smaller, lighter, and more powerful with improved user interfaces—not unlike what we experienced with phones and computers. And he predicts that cloud computing and streaming will make devices even more user friendly and valuable because the processing of information will no longer rely on bandwidth and Wi-Fi. This is particularly important as we begin transmitting more spatial data because this requires high bandwidth.

AI workflows are also front of mind. These enable people to build no-code interfaces on spatial computing sources. This will allow instructors the ability to create and share content in real time to learners for a specific circumstance or simulation. Then AI-generated content acts as a constant data source of relevant information that adapts with the learner, so every individual has a more personalized learning experience.

Another cool thing is that as XR devices evolve, they will be able to capture more sensory information that can be sent back to the spatial computing source, which can in turn change the content for learners. This is the beauty of the intersection of XR and AI.

When asked specifically how these tech trends would impact learning and learners, Gates mentioned that this is the first time humans will be able to create infinite amounts of personalization without sacrificing scale. To date, learning leaders have had to choose if they want to zero in on mass personalization or mass scale, but not both at the same time.

SO WHAT? NOW WHAT?

If you take anything away from this chapter, it's that we will continue to see the emergence of new technologies as well as the convergence of technologies. The pace at which this is all thrown at us can indeed be a little daunting. I think what can feel unsettling is that our foundation of teaching and learning is no longer made of bedrock. That has gone the way of Fred Flintstone. Our foundation more closely resembles a floating floor with interlocking pieces that can be upgraded or replaced over time. A floor is still under our feet, but the components are constantly changing at differing points of time.

The support system remains, but the colors, textures, materials, and density are changing. Understanding that some of these pieces become worn or outdated over time and can be replaced with better pieces might help make sense of this constant transition we find ourselves in. As long as a support system is paired with a robust strategy, we are all capable of handling technological change with confidence and an open mindset. And the key is to change these pieces proactively rather than reactively.

At the heart of it, providing students and employees with learning opportunities is a service. And it is our responsibility to deliver these services that best support our customers and to prepare them for a world of fast-paced change, emerging technologies, and managing the unknown. Imagine if we were still teaching our students to learn math using an abacus. Or handwriting lessons on a blackboard with chalk. Or teaching shorthand. Or teaching how to set up handwritten ledgers. Each of these "tools" was replaced by something much more efficient and convenient, thanks to emerging technology. At the time, people may have hesitated to do things in a different way, but streamlining these processes or roles enabled us to do other things with our time.

Unfortunately, or fortunately, we all need to evolve and adapt as human beings to the fast-evolving world around us. No one is immune. We're not just talking about technology or learning. Steve Grubbs of VictoryXR reinforced this point by stating that the improvements and confluence of emerging technologies are going to impact us on a societal level in addition to learning over the next five years. While we may want to hold on to certain traditions (understandably so), ignoring external factors such as technological evolution is not a wise strategy. Plus, without adapting to change, you render yourself obsolete, which is what so many people are trying to avoid by continuing to do what they've always done. Ironic.

To be clear, you don't need to be a "techie" or have a background in STEM to embrace technology in learning. Yogini and I are a case in point. Yogini's liberal arts doctorate and technology might seem like unlikely bedfellows, but it is precisely this "nontechnical" education that helps her make connections between subject matter expertise, desired client outcomes, and technology-enhanced, experiential learning.

As an entrepreneurship professor-turned-entrepreneur, I brought my expertise around innovation and problem solving into founding a tech startup. The introduction to immersive technology was our "aha" moment as we fell in love with the promise of VR to create engaging, inclusive, experiential learning. Soon, we were soaking up techspeak, collaborating with partners on their VR design and development turf, and carving out our own little niche in the forthcoming metaverse.

One thing to avoid is adopting new technology because it's shiny and new or because it has the cool factor. Have a well-drafted strategy for which technologies make most sense for your organization, and be willing to change that strategy along the way. Keep those floor puzzle pieces in mind. Technology can become an enabler of transformational and experiential learning, which we have shown to be impactful, engaging, and meaningful for adult learners. At the same time, we need to be mindful of not using technology for technology's sake and falling into a digital version of our age-old status quo. Technology in a vacuum cannot transform learning, but learning leaders can create systems for deploying technological tools to create learner-centric, experiential, inquiry-based learning environments (Meier et al. 2023).

CHAPTER 9

The Imaginary Box

ORIGINATION OF THE BOX

Have you ever attempted the nine dots puzzle? It's a classic lateral thinking exercise that was popular in the mid to late 1990s, but its origins trace back to Sam Loyd, a puzzle author, in the mid-nineteenth century (Art of Play 2016). The proposition is this: You are presented with nine dots laid out in a three-by-three grid on a piece of paper as seen below. The goal is to connect all nine dots using four straight lines (or fewer!) without lifting your writing utensil off the page.

Grab a piece of paper, and give it a try before turning the page. The answer is on the other side.

Here's the answer (well, *one* of the answers):

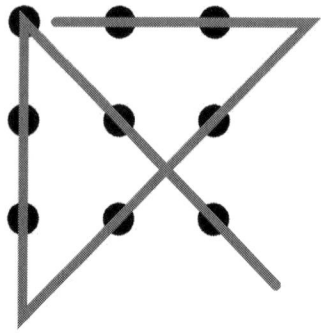

Most people can't solve this because they immediately assume you have to remain within the confines of the outer border created by the dots. *Why do people make this assumption?* The instructions are straightforward and don't present any restrictions or limitations aside from keeping your writing utensil on the page. It's fascinating to observe people trying to figure this out and the discussions that come along with it. This is where the concept of thinking inside and outside the box comes from. Thinking "inside" the box is constrained and narrow-minded, whereas thinking "outside" the box is associated with being opportunistic and creative.

The crazy thing is not only do we speak about *thinking* inside/outside the box, but we also act on it. For example, we put people in brainstorming sessions to think outside the box. When we are pressed to be more innovative, it's time to think outside the box! It's as if the normal, day-to-day way of being and thinking is inside the box and thus narrow-minded. And there's a lot of truth to that. Most people like to operate in a space and frame of mind that is comfortable and familiar. Because going outside that comfort zone is, well, uncomfortable. So using this box metaphor is in complete alignment with one's comfort zone. Get out of your comfort zone!

Here's the thing: These are both man-made concepts that impact our thoughts and actions. This box and this zone don't exist. It's all in our heads. It is a state of mind. And because of this mindset, too many people go through life unable to unleash creativity and realize opportunity. What would happen if we removed these mental barriers? (Insert mind-blowing emoji.)

Frankly, I'm not impressed when people say they are thinking outside the box, as if that warrants a ticker tape parade. This is the space and mindset we should always operate in. Why not? Will we be punished for being too creative? Are we going to gain ten pounds for being deft and agile? Has anyone ever been arrested for being ingenious? What's the hold up? Our minds are guiding our actions, so my proposition is that we open up our minds to new possibilities and begin making this the norm.

Hear ye! Hear ye! Gone be the box!

OPEN MINDS AND OPEN SPACES
Without question, one of the first things we need to do is remove barriers—whether they be mental, physical, emotional, organizational, systemic, or societal. Certainly, removing clutter in a physical space or eliminating outdated policies in the workplace will take a little work, but the new "space"

will create a sense of openness and freedom. And yes, *some* barriers will be more difficult to discard than others, so let's first focus on the low hanging fruit that we *can* control: mental barriers.

When I used to teach entrepreneurship to college students, we regularly talked about getting out of one's comfort zone—because that's where the opportunities lie. By definition, entrepreneurship is about coming up with a novel solution to address a problem. If we are going to be opportunistic problem solvers as entrepreneurs, then we have to go beyond our normal thought processes and do something different than what currently exists. We often discussed pushing oneself to the point of failure because we learn so much more from our mistakes than our successes, as mentioned in a prior chapter. Here's one of my favorite examples I used to share with my students:

> Raise your hand if you are a gym rat, or at least regularly engage in some sort of weight-bearing exercise. (Me, me, me!)
>
> When you first start lifting weights, you're introduced to the typical regimen of doing X sets of Y reps with Z amount of weight. It's very common to knock out three sets of twelve to fifteen reps with, say, twenty-pound dumbbells, or some variation of that.
>
> Now, I have regularly observed people at the gym and even my own habits, and I have come to the realization that if you stay confined within these parameters and get comfortable with a certain

routine, you won't see much change or progress. Your muscles won't be challenged anymore. They aren't stimulated.

Let's look at what bodybuilders do. They subscribe to a weightlifting strategy known as "lifting to failure" or "pushing to failure." This entails knocking out as many reps as possible until you can't do one more; you've reached muscular failure. *That* is when you see major progress.

Here's why weightlifting is so beneficial: Weight bearing exercises can result in microscopic tears in the tiny fibers in our muscles. And this is a good thing because the body automatically repairs these tears and, in doing so, makes the muscles stronger and in many cases bigger. This process is called hypertrophy.

The lesson: If we want to see real progress, we need to stretch ourselves to reach new goals. Regularly pushing ourselves to failure will result in attaining our full potential.

I would argue that we should apply this same strategy of pushing to failure to stretch our minds. Think of this as mental hypertrophy. But if we play it safe and settle into a comfortable, standard routine, things are going to get stale. We don't see substantive change. Our brains aren't stimulated. Unfortunately, this is the state where most of us operate. What if we specifically approached learning with this pushing-to-failure mindset?

The amazing thing is that we don't have a mental tipping point. Thinking and creativity do not have a failure point or maximum threshold. *We* are the ones who put up imaginary constraints. So not only do we as learning leaders need to open up our minds to possibilities of teaching, but we also need to encourage this same mindset in our learners. (I'm getting goosebumps just thinking about the infinite change this could spark in so many people.)

Speaking of goosebumps, about ten to eleven years ago, I was researching schools for my daughter who would be entering elementary school. In our neighborhood in Connecticut was a small private school that really sparked my curiosity, so I booked an appointment with the director of admissions. It goes without saying the environment and teaching philosophies were exceptional. Since my daughter would soon be entering kindergarten, we zoned in on that part of the building. As nearly every school does, written stories and artwork created by students were showcased on the walls outside many of the classrooms. I stopped at one of the bulletin boards and began reading one short story after another and was shocked to find out that these had been written by five-year-olds. Five! These kids weren't confined to learning simple ABCs. They were already writing in full sentences and putting creative thoughts together. I was floored.

This is the perfect example of giving people (even young people!) the permission to flourish. They weren't put in the same box and regimen as every other elementary school that dictates in this grade you learn this (no more, no less), and in this grade you learn this. Everyone is learning in lockstep and not given much opportunity to go beyond state mandates for each grade. How dumb is this? What if we nurtured kids to push as far as they could go when learning? Imagine if we allowed them to learn at their own pace and not be held back by constraints. Imagine if kids weren't taught in the confines of this imaginary box. Imagine the potential.

These kindergartners have no idea what thinking inside/outside of the box is. It doesn't exist for them. So, if *they* can learn with an open mindset, why can't we as adults? Well, we have to start by getting rid of borders and outdated systems.

THE VALUE OF FAILURE AND REGRET
A few years ago, Yogini was teaching a business negotiation course at a university in California. One of her students, let's call her Jayna, reacted with abrasion every time an interactive exercise involved personal and professional negotiation scenarios. "Winning at all costs!" she wrote when asked about her learning goals at the beginning of the term. She believed that conceding anything or considering the negotiation counterparty's point of view was unacceptable. Her fear of failure was the foundation for those emotions and reactions.

Atychiphobia is the unwarranted and chronic fear of making any kind of mistake. This phobia stifles between 2 and 5 percent of the population (Hill 2018). Within the context of learning, this can be crippling—mentally, emotionally, and physically. Sure, some amount of fear might be motivating for learning and growth. For example, a fear of failure may motivate learners to make a study schedule, complete their work on time, or strive for top grades. However, a fear of failure can also make it difficult to make good decisions. At work, fear of failure can have debilitating social and financial consequences, as it might pigeonhole employees as incapable or unworthy of promotions. So, what can you do if your learners are mired in the box and afraid to make mistakes?

Educators and trainers can make all the difference by empowering learners to confront, process, and even embrace failure. Dr. Carol Dweck, renowned psychologist and professor at Stanford University, famously coined the term "growth mindset," suggesting that this is a state of mind whereby people are open to change. Her book entitled *Mindset: The New Psychology of Success* states that success is about stretching beyond the comfort zone (or the box!), learning, and improving. Failure is an opportunity to learn (2006).

Dweck presents a powerful case for learners to alter their mindsets as well. This one really resonated with me because of my personal experience learning a new language.

> [Imagine] you're in a language class [where] the instructor calls on you and starts throwing questions at you one after another. Put yourself in a fixed mindset. Your ability is on the line. Can you feel everyone's eyes on you? Feel the tension, feel your ego bristle and waver. Now put yourself in a growth mindset. You're a novice—that's why you're here. You're here to learn. The teacher is a resource for learning. Feel the tension leave you; feel your mind open up. The message is: you can change your mindset (Dweck 2006).

Additionally, with a growth mindset, you give yourself permission to fail and the room to stretch yourself into discomfort even (or especially) when it's not going well.

Building off failure, we can also look at the concept of regret. One of Daniel Pink's books, *The Power of Regret: How Looking Backward Moves Us Forward*, offers the counterintuitive viewpoint of regret as a learning mechanism. Pink says that even in the workplace, regrets don't need to be hidden or brushed off simply because they are uncomfortable to face. "They [regrets] are also our most transformative [negative emotions] in that if we deal with them properly, they can help us in a whole array of areas, particularly in business, [for example] to make better decisions. They can help us become better negotiators, better problem solvers, and better strategists if we treat them right" (2022).

Yogini is a big fan of Pink's book. Her favorite part of the book is the concept of a failure résumé. Imagine if our résumés highlighted our failures instead of our successes, and interviewees focused on all the lessons learned from their mistakes and failures. I love this idea. Instead of "no regrets" as the best corporate badge to wear, what if leaders stared regrets in the eye and had honest, authentic conversations with their team about regrets? Pink writes, "There's even evidence—and I think a lot of leaders don't get this because it's counterintuitive—that disclosing those regrets and mistakes actually strengthens your standing and builds affinity rather than the reverse" (2022).

Back to Jayna. Thankfully, her story ends on a happy note. Having talked through her fear of failure, she made a three-part plan to become a better negotiator by not always "winning."

Step one: She gave herself permission to be vulnerable. Step two: She listened to the counterparty and thought of negotiation as a joint success. Step three: She focused on relationships, not just transactions. When the semester ended, she was voted the most empowered learner in the class.

Today's lesson: While concepts such as failure and regret are perceived as negative things, experimenting and making mistakes have so much value with respect to learning. Giving learners permission to push themselves outside their comfort zones presents endless amounts of potential and can dramatically change both their perceptions about learning and learning outcomes.

EMPOWERING LEARNING PROFESSIONALS

"Those who can, do. Those who can't, teach." This famous quote from George Bernard Shaw really rankled Yogini for a long time. What lies behind this impression that teachers exude? Yogini, for one, is the first to admit that she fails regularly at negotiating, one of the business subjects she teaches. Either a deal doesn't go the way she wants, or she walks away from a negotiation having learned some insightful lessons about relationships and transactions. And that's not a bad thing.

She uses these mistakes as opportunities for improvement. She holds up her negotiation failures to scrutiny in class with her students and develops strategies together to better prepare for the next negotiation. She does better with business negotiations because of this reflection, and in turn she helps her students understand that negotiating is an art, not a science, and that learning never ends.

It takes courage to admit failure, imperfection, and vulnerability. Brené Brown hosted a TED talk on "The Power of Vulnerability" back in 2011. In it, she shares her research on the subject and says that (1) acknowledging our fears and imperfections, (2) embracing our vulnerability, and (3) leaning into our frailties actually helps us grow and evolve. Being in this state also allows us to connect with others from a more authentic place. So, it's time to loosen up a bit. Start with yourself when it comes to unboxing our limitations and fears.

What are instructors afraid of? Fear of control comes to mind, which can take the form of fear of losing track of the lesson plan, fear of losing their place of power, fear of not knowing enough, or fear of their students knowing more than they do. And yet embracing this fear and uncertainty demonstrates to our learners we are co-travelers in a VUCA (volatile, uncertain, complex, ambiguous) world and offers "teachable moments" to demonstrate how to embrace uncertainty and change.

Yogini recalled shuddering at the thought of losing control when she was a new teacher. To her, it reflected a failing within her, or affirmed the niggling self-doubt of not being good enough to teach a subject she was still mastering (German, in her case, the fourth language she had started learning as a teenager). It was only a few semesters in that she found the confidence to share her learning journey with students as a way of encouraging them to see the possibilities with language learning in a kind of if-I-can-do-it-so-can-you, inspiration-rousing effort.

And sometimes, that's all it takes. More than threats of grades or discipline, it is the instructor's ability to embrace a little chaos and let go of their place in the classroom hierarchy that connects with learners. An *Education Week* article explains, "Once we accept that control is really just a unicorn of stories of the past, we can truly embrace the beauty of allowing students to be empowered, with us at their sides helping them to harness all that they have before them" (Sackstein 2019). Appropriately, the Greek goddess of Chaos, or Khaos, symbolizes formless and infinite space. What if we seized chaos with open arms and in turn made learning experiences formless and infinite? (Insert mind-blowing emoji.)

LEARNING EVERYWHERE

One of the more obvious—and detrimental—constraints we see when it comes to learning is the limitations of a physical classroom and the standard setup of the space. Formal, interactive learning no longer needs to be delivered in a traditional classroom on a campus or in a training environment in the workplace. This is very much an inside-the-box experience.

Certainly, being in the same space with others for learning purposes has its benefits. One hundred percent. But must it always be in a physical space? Learners are often faced with their own set of restrictions given their personal lives, such as geographical barriers or family responsibilities. What if teachers/trainers and learners could gather in a whole new virtual dimension and learn together from anywhere?

We can now expand the conversation from "people can access learning from wherever they are" to "people can be transported to different spaces and timeframes to learn everywhere." It *is* possible. Today. Now. Cutting-edge virtual platforms and software have become more mainstream for true immersive learning. The result is experiential learning on steroids. In many cases, all learners need is a VR headset and Wi-Fi to literally learn from anywhere—with others from every corner of the world in a 3D environment.

Even if in-person training is preferred at your organization, virtual learning environments provide a supplemental source that learners can access 24-7 to practice and refine skills they learned in class. They can continue to learn in solo or social situations—from home or their own office or while on vacation—well after their formal training has ended.

In addition, when we say "learning everywhere," immersive learning tools leveraged in VR, for example, can open a time capsule. We can take learners inside the human body, to the moon, to exotic lands, and to historical sites that have been recreated to appear like they did decades or centuries ago. The physical and time barriers are removed, thus opening up significantly more information and experiences than we could ever access before.

SO WHAT? NOW WHAT?

Now that we are aware of the constraints of "the box" and "the zone," let's eliminate them. There's no use for either of them. They suppress us from reaching our full potential as well as that of those we serve in our profession. By now, I hope you see what you've been missing and perhaps more importantly *why* you've been thinking and acting within the confines of this man-made conceptual box. No finger wagging here. It is just a realization that we as human beings act and think in ways that are familiar.

According to Dr. Gary Klein of *Psychology Today*, our mindsets are rooted in our beliefs. Beliefs and values are difficult to alter because we have learned them from our environments, our childhood, our role models, our cultures, etc., and they have become ingrained in who we are (2023). So, changing our mindset requires a fundamental change in ourselves and an openness to the fact that perhaps some of the things we thought or believed in the past might not lead to the best mindset for our personal growth. Mindsets are very powerful and can lead us to both positive and negative outcomes. The onus is on us to *at the very least* be open to possibilities and alternatives.

It's time for the rubber to meet the road and take action. One of the most overused—and underutilized—words in business today is "agile." People like to throw that one around as much as "innovation." (Insert eyeroll emoji.) In addition, promises of developing "critical thinkers" and "problem solvers" are overused within the world of higher education. Folks, there's a lot of window dressing, but we're not going beyond the standard and usual. We're never going to be any of those things without radically changing both our mindsets and behaviors.

Yes, of course, some institutions are fortunate to have visionary leaders or bulging endowments that provide the opportunity to be change agents, but the proportion of these to the number of education institutions is slim. The same thing applies to companies. Some cutting-edge, tech-driven organizations are leading the pack (FYI, you can find most of these on the Nasdaq stock exchange), but when you look under the hood of most companies, they are far from agile and innovative. I suspect most are playing within the confines of the box or just stuck in the traditional ways of being and doing, à la "That's how we've always done it."

When I was interviewing Corey Mohn of CAPS, we were talking about this conceptual box so many people are trapped in. To my surprise (well, not really... I'm speaking with Corey Mohn), he reached over to a table near his desk and showed me a medium-sized white box he had nearby. Printed on the top was "Most people try to get outside the box." When he opened the box, another statement was printed on the inside: "CAPS destroys the box." *Shazam!* Music to my ears. That credo and mindset are clearly baked into the culture of CAPS, but it's also a way of living and being for Corey, his team, and his students.

Like any change management effort, we need to go through a process:

1. Understand the what/where/why/when of the *current* state of learning;
2. Understand the what/where/why/when of the *desired* state of learning; and
3. Understand the process for said transition.

The process piece is critical. We need buy-in from people who will be affected by the change. They need to know what's in it for them and how much effort it will take to go through the transition. And more importantly, they need to understand *why* the change is happening.

Start opening your mind to the possibilities of teaching and training without the guardrails, even though having too much space can sometimes feel daunting. It can be difficult to know how or where to start, but it is a liberating transformation. So your mission, should you choose to accept, is to get rid of the box and all the baggage that goes along with it. This might require a little sweat, but the results will be worth it.

CHAPTER 10

Learning Rewired at Edstutia

THE CATALYST

I launched my EdTech company, Edstutia, back in 2020. You might think the time was ripe because I had extra time on my hands due to the pandemic, but it was more like the pandemic pushed me forward because of what I experienced as an educator. No words can explain the massive disruption we all experienced, but in my small corner of the world, I was also feeling and observing the impact this virus had on the entire ecosystem of academia.

I was still teaching in higher education when the pandemic hit and everyone rallied to finish up the semester with some semblance of normalcy. Personally, I was prepared for whatever the pandemic dealt us. My curriculum and teaching style were already pretty fluid. I *loved* the fact this historical event forced educators to learn how to utilize more technology. Sadly, most professors are rather complacent and not very tech savvy, so it was interesting to observe how my peers and, frankly, the entire industry struggled with adopting new tech skills. A *lot* of emotions were tied to the demands put upon us with the accelerated tech adoption—frustration, exhaustion, caution, and fear—but it was technology that saved us during this time. Technology enabled us to keep communicating and connecting and working together.

> **Pop quiz:** Had you used or even heard of Zoom before the pandemic? Look where we are today. As of February 2025, an average of three hundred million users are on Zoom every single day (Woodward 2025). Say what?

While we were in the thick of pandemic transition time, I recall thinking, *How do we get people to continue moving forward with technology after realizing its benefits? How do we keep that curiosity alive to continue learning about emerging technologies to make our personal and professional lives better?* And by better, I mean more collaborative, more meaningful, more interactive, more exciting, and yes—more fun. It was no time to rest on our laurels.

Back to Edstutia. I built an immersive learning company that is at the forefront of rewiring learning as we know it today. Our focus is on adult learning, which includes professional development for employees in the workplace and learning experiences for students at higher education institutions. We initially started with one windowless room in VR and then designed an entire campus to support both solo and social learning, and to provide a wider variety of learning environments. We develop content for end users as well as training courses to educate learning leaders about extended reality (XR) and AI and the value they bring to the learning experience.

The crises listed in chapter 3 led me to leave my job in higher education to jump into uncharted territory. I wanted to build an education business that had the potential to reach way more students and address the skills gap. I was on a mission to drive some real change akin to the Uber story.

THE VISION

My original vision was to create an alternative university that went head-to-head with higher education institutions. I was so fed up with the status quo of the rising cost of tuition, the mountains of student loan debt young people are buried under, the perpetual skills gap, and the lack of agility and tech adoption at colleges and universities. Clearly some parties benefit from the existing systems and processes so prevalent in higher ed, but my heart bleeds for the students and their families who are bending over backward to send their high school graduates to college.

I began my journey by speaking to industry experts to find out what skills they were looking for, especially with new college graduates. I wanted to make sure what I was creating was of value to them. I wanted to focus on preparing young people, military veterans, and career changers on in-demand skills for in-demand industries such as big data and cybersecurity. I wanted to make apprenticeships cool again and carve out a direct pipeline between students and employers. I wanted to get rid of tests and grades, focusing solely on experiential learning. I really wanted to turn the existing model of higher education upside down and give people an alternative to getting buried in debt.

Long story short, that B2C model is on ice waiting to be resurrected someday. I pivoted about a year and a half later to a B2B business model. Our target audience shifted to corporate learning leaders in L&D, human resources, talent management, and DEIB, as well as professors and leaders in higher education. My underlying vision and fire in the belly remain, but I now want to provide immersive learning products and services to those who are learning professionals and their learners. And… I also want to be the go-to source for helping people understand the purpose, value, and benefits of immersive learning and to embrace emerging technology.

THE PURPOSE

Returning to chapter 1 and leveraging my modern-day definition of the purpose of learning, I walk the walk by integrating this belief into what I have built with Edstutia. The purpose of Edstutia is to provide engaging, immersive, experiential learning using cutting edge technology to prepare students, employees, and companies for what lies ahead. To be tech savvy. To be open minded. To be adaptive. To reignite a love of learning in people. To think about learning without traditional parameters or confines.

I am a big proponent of experiential learning. Aside from the content and activities, it was critical we created a low-risk, safe space with different learning environments to provide authentic learning experiences that included making mistakes. Sitting in a classroom or on a Zoom session isn't the right environment for experiential learning. Learners need the opportunity to learn by doing. Taking all the benefits of experiential learning and combining these with all the possibilities of immersive technology is like explosive combustion. The possibilities are endless—and that's why this is so exciting.

THE IMPACT

We are in the midst of sorting through somewhat of a mash-up of emerging technologies that are downright disruptive. For some people, this is a threat. For others (like me), I see the disruption as a positive thing because our learners deserve a better experience, period. Since Edstutia doesn't exist as a physical brick-and-mortar entity and our overhead remains low, we are not stuck like other education departments and institutions. In the virtual world, we can adapt our venues and environments at any time for a fraction of the cost and time. We can add infinite spaces and experiences to the campus. And we can seamlessly integrate new technologies—those that don't even exist today—onto our campus when necessary. The bottom line is we can be much more agile and adaptive than education institutions or corporate universities.

How does this impact our key constituents?

The impact to learners	Convenient, action-oriented, relevant, efficient, engaging content that breeds lifelong learning.
The impact on learning leaders	New tools and opportunities to significantly improve learner outcomes and to gain a competitive edge.
The impact on higher education	Access to cutting edge tools and resources to stay relevant and better serve next-gen students.
The impact on organizations	New, affordable options to keep employees up to speed with in-demand skills and mindsets.

OUR DIFFERENTIATORS

In addition to having an entire virtual campus with a variety of venues, learning environments for solo and social learning, and learner functionality, here are some other ways we set ourselves apart:

1. **FOCUS ON BUSINES, LEADERSHIP, AND PEOPLE-CENTRIC SKILLS**: Why focus on these skills? Because we did our homework and conducted research with hiring managers across multiple industries to find out what skills they were looking for in employees. Across the board, employers are in desperate need of people who are exceptional problem solvers, leaders, and communicators who are resilient and agile. This is the sweet spot.

2. **ASSESSMENT**: We don't assess learners in traditional ways. We don't administer tests. We don't give grades. All learning is experiential learning, and learners are able to demonstrate their newly acquired skills through hands-on projects and tangible deliverables. We also capture learner feedback along the way to identify any gaps in learning. This iterative process enables us to adjust our content in real time if necessary and make sure everyone is making the expected advancements.

3. **PROPRIETARY DASHBOARD**: We gather learner data from the VR headsets, from within VR via hotspots and surveys and from our learning experience portal (LXP). This triangulation of data ensures we are capturing a more comprehensive and accurate picture of each learner's progress. All this data is aggregated into

our proprietary dashboard, which showcases learner confidence levels, technology fluency, knowledge gain, and practical application. No smiley faces.

4. **XR-CERTIFIED INSTRUCTORS**: My core team and instructors are also seasoned professionals with many years of experience in teaching, training, and coaching on business and "power" skills. All have completed our XR certification program, so they understand immersive technologies and how to utilize them specifically for adult learning. They know how to create meaningful content and activities in VR for value-add learning experiences. This is our Good Housekeeping stamp of approval to the world that our instructors know how to best utilize XR tools for learning purposes.

5. **ADA COMPLIANCE**: We have added features and controls that are in compliance with the Americans with Disabilities Act (ADA), thus ensuring that everyone can experience Edstutia regardless of most physical impairments or constraints. Taking into consideration a variety of disabilities, we added new features to our campus such as: closed captioning, audio controls, clear color indicators, custom hand controller settings, and the ability to resize assets such as 3D models. In addition, we have a desktop version of the campus for people who can't or don't want to wear a headset. Mission: no learner left behind.

6. **LIVE INSTRUCTOR-LED MODULES**: Most of our modules are synchronous sessions led by subject matter experts. Simply creating prerecorded simulations

or self-directed learning modules misses the point of utilizing immersive technology and optimizing experiential learning. The opportunity to interact with others from around the world in real time, in a new dimension, creates an authentic, engaging experience with real impact.

7. **ARTIFICIAL INTELLIGENCE**: With the integration of custom AI features, we can conduct simulations and roleplays with AI-engineered avatars that have personalities, attitudes, emotions, body language, and more. This empowers users to have a more realistic, free-flowing conversation with infinite outcomes versus an interaction that is scripted and predictable. AI can also knock out an assessment report in a fraction of the time it would take an instructor with preset rubrics, criteria, and measurements—which are also customizable.

WHO'S IN THE DRIVER'S SEAT?

Everything we have presented so far in this book are things Yogini and I believe in and practice ourselves. We also understand that learners are the focal point. They *have to be*.

We have seen other industries disrupted once customers were in the driver's seat. Take the marketing and advertising industries. We *used to* live in a world where the marketers would influence us to buy their products, and our only options were what was on the shelves at our local retailers. Take it or leave it. The product or service providers had the power. Their job was to convince and entice us to open our wallets.

Enter the internet and social media, and all of a sudden fifteen-year-old Isabella from a small town near Cleveland, Ohio, has more power and influence than conceivable with her TikTok videos. She can make or break your brand and reputation. Marketers and companies are forced to pay attention and adapt.

I previously mentioned how Uber disrupted the cab industry. It took an outlier to drive change in an antiquated, complacent industry. If it weren't for Uber, we would still be dealing with subpar, overpriced, intermittent transportation. The power is in the hands of innovators and consumers. Incumbents have the same opportunities in front of them as do the disrupters. The difference lies in one's mindset. Too many organizations operate from a place of complacency, which often leads to the biggest problems in the eyes of consumers, students, and employees. This also leads to massive opportunities for the entrepreneurs and innovators of the world who see things differently, who identify a worthwhile problem to solve, and who have identified a large enough market of people looking for new alternatives.

In our world, the power should be—and is!—transitioning from the service providers (e.g., higher education, educators, trainers) to the customers (students, employees, learners). Show me any other successful business or industry that doesn't put their customers first. Why should education and training be any different? If learners can find what they need elsewhere, they will. And so, the seismic shift begins. Edstutia was designed to serve learners (a.k.a. customers) who are looking for a better option than what's on the dusty bookshelves today.

THE IMMERSIVE LEARNING EXPERIENCE AT EDSTUTIA
Learning in VR is the exemplification of "there is no box" learning. Why? Because it transcends the boundaries of time and space with its ability to put learners in a leadership coaching scenario on a Mount Everest climb, health care professionals inside the human body or inside patient experiences such as someone suffering from Alzheimer's, and allowing students to interact with AI bots of historical figures such as Abraham Lincoln or Marie Curie.

What is it like to learn in a virtual space? Without experiencing it yourself firsthand, it's not easy to comprehend, but let me share a few examples.

ROLEPLAYING IN A BOARDROOM
Take the scenario of being in a professional boardroom to practice skills like interview prep, negotiation, or de-escalating a heated argument. As avatars, you can take on multiple roles to build empathy and understanding. The environment is authentic and a safe space to make mistakes. Learners can practice such scenarios as much as they need to until they've reached a level of confidence and are ready to apply their newly acquired skills in the real world. Adding AI-engineered avatars as nonplayer characters (NPCs) takes things to another level by engaging learners in a non-scripted, free-flowing dialogue. With a record and playback feature, learners can reflect, observe, and even get real-time coaching to round out the lesson.

COLLABORATION IN THE MAIN HALL

Our Main Hall is a large, open space that is great for collaboration, group work, brainstorming, and more. Typical exercises in this space might be games that utilize AR or audio files to add another dimension to the learning. Spawning assets such as 3D objects and whiteboards are great tools for explaining concepts as well as understanding and appreciating different perspectives in your group. Having tangible tools paired with a true sense of presence makes the interactive part of VR come alive when you realize you are interacting with people from all over the world in a different dimension. Try doing that on Zoom.

360 IMMERSIONS IN THE EXPLORATORY

The Exploratory is our most futuristic venue on campus and was designed to be a space for self-discovery. The main feature of the Exploratory is six theaters that house 360-degree immersions. Being able to transport learners to different spaces and eras is powerful. We have used this type of immersion to teach cultural nuances by taking people to marketplaces in different parts of the world. Obviously this is either cost prohibitive or impossible to do in the real world, so it is a cost-effective way to experience a different space or time. The sights, sounds, and energy feel real. It's not a flat experience but one that is much more sensory in nature.

What are customers saying about their experiences on the Edstutia platform?

Maria Zevaoglu
Intercultural Communications Specialist

"Before taking the immersive learning course in extended reality (XR), I had a limited understanding of the potential and applications of virtual reality (VR) and XR technologies. My experience was mostly limited to basic interactions and surface-level knowledge. However, this course has truly transformed my perspective.

"From the very start, the course offered a highly engaging introduction to XR. The content was well-structured, providing a comprehensive overview that made complex concepts accessible. The blend of theoretical knowledge with practical, hands-on activities was particularly effective for me.

"One specific highlight of the course was the immersive simulation exercises. These activities allow us to experience VR environments firsthand, offering a practical and memorable way to understand different levels of virtual interactions. This element not only enhanced the learning experience but also demonstrated the possible applications of XR in a way that was both educational and exciting.

"Overall, this course is an excellent starting point for anyone new to VR and XR. It stands out for its engaging content, practical approach, and the effective use of immersive simulations to bring the material to life. I highly recommend it for those looking to gain a solid foundation in extended reality. It not only demystified, but also equipped me with foundational skills that are essential for navigating and leveraging these technologies. By the way, the Edstutia campus is amazing!"

Jennifer William, PhD
Head of the School of Languages and Cultures
Purdue University

"We've been getting into [virtual reality] in languages and cultures at Purdue over the past few years, and we have taken advantage of some of Edstutia's instructor training options. We have found them to be fantastic and hope to do more! This is a great option to consider to help take teaching tech skills to instructors to the next level. Edstutia has my ringing endorsement [for] universities who might benefit from these kinds of training and consulting services for immersive learning."

Jennifer Neumaier, EdD
Founder, Connected Collective
Director, University of Pennsylvania's
Chief Learning Officer Executive Doctoral Program

"In my work, I have seen firsthand the power of connection in driving organizational success, and Edstutia's groundbreaking VR technology has elevated this to an entirely new level. Traditional virtual meetings lack the depth of human connection needed to foster meaningful relationships, but Edstutia's immersive environments create a dynamic, three-dimensional space where employees can engage, learn, and build trust—no matter where they are in the world.

"As someone who specializes in creating the connective tissue within organizations, I have integrated Edstutia's platform into my work and witnessed remarkable transformations. Teams that once struggled with isolation and disengagement have found new energy, collaboration, and a sense of belonging through interactive, thoughtfully designed VR experiences. This technology has not only enhanced communication but has also deepened learning, strengthened culture, and ultimately driven measurable results. Edstutia is not just redefining virtual engagement; it is revolutionizing the way people connect, and I am proud to have seen its profound impact firsthand.

"Even though I was a bit fearful of the technology at first, I enrolled in their XR certification course and was blown away by this experience! I came away thinking I could really accomplish anything using VR. As for Edstutia's expertise… if it's out of ten, I'd say they're one hundred. They empowered me to do great things."

SO WHAT? NOW WHAT?

We are in the early stages of this new tech cycle with immersive technologies. It will morph and improve throughout its thirty-plus-year cycle and will eventually become the norm for how we learn (among other uses). Since launching Edstutia, the technology has improved significantly—from the avatars to the headsets to new functionality. And we have adapted accordingly in response to our target audience's requests and needs. To date, we have spent an inordinate amount of time educating people about the world of immersive learning and getting them acclimated to using the technology for learning purposes. We'll look back five years from now and wonder why it was so difficult to transition to XR.

The purpose of sharing the example of Edstutia is two-fold: (1) to illustrate what's possible when the box disappears; and (2) to inspire you to start thinking like a disruptor, like an innovator, like a game changer. Every person and organization is privy to the same options on the table: either be disrupted or be the disruptor. By altering our attitudes and perspectives, we can drive all sorts of ingenuity.

Let's begin by changing our perspectives and attitudes to take advantage of all the amazing opportunities at this point in time. Blockbuster innovations like the internet, XR, and AI don't come along every day. Don't wake up someday saying "coulda, shoulda, woulda." Small steps, everyone…

FROM	TO
"That will never happen."	"I want to be a part of what's happening."
"We've been doing X like this for a long time. Why change now?"	"We've been doing X like this for too long. We better change now or become irrelevant."
"We are the experts. We know best."	"Let's listen to our customers/learners to find out what they want."
"Things need to be standardized to measure and compare outcomes."	"Adaptive and customized learning experiences will result in better outcomes."
"Trying new technology is a waste of time and money."	"Let's reallocate our resources to invest in value-add technologies for a competitive advantage."

Given how much Edstutia has changed since its inception, I can't even imagine what the platform will look like five years from now. I find that uncertainty exciting, and I know it will evolve in cadence with emerging technology and learner expectations.

CHAPTER 11

Unboxing

with Sanika Doolani, PhD

LET THE SHIFT HIT THE FAN

Throughout this book, we have clearly laid out where and why change needs to happen. While our interest and focus are definitely with adult learners, breaking out of the box applies to all kinds of learners/learning, including K–12 and even homeschooling. We are all on a learning continuum that never really stops. Well, it shouldn't. So why wait until someone is in college to start adopting our proposed mindset? Also, what we are proposing here isn't just for learning. A renewed mindset can be applied to every aspect of one's life—from how we tackle goals such as preparing to run a marathon or diving into a new culture.

I'm going to steal a few things from Tony Robbins, the globally renowned speaker and author. He is the epitome of a transformational speaker who helps people transform their lives for the better. On his website, he has a page dedicated to "How to Create Positive Energy." The first thing on his list is

"Shift your mindset." "Creating positive energy is all about your state of mind. You must take responsibility for yourself and your life and truly commit to changing your perspective. Stop looking at life from a place of fear or anger and begin to identify the limiting beliefs and negative patterns that are preventing you from living with joy" (Robbins n.d.). (We can easily equate this to how we approach our profession and responsibilities.)

I hope you have already begun stretching your mind while reading this book. Why not make a deliberate shift and hold yourself accountable? Make a point to begin embracing things, such as:

- Emerging technology
- Experiential learning
- Learner-centric transformational learning
- Boldly questioning the status quo
- Taking risks
- Mistakes and failure
- Adopting, adapting, and agility
- Learner agency
- Lifelong learning

Feeling overwhelmed? Unsure where to start? Ask yourself and others lots of "why" questions as a baseline. If you haven't already read Simon Sinek's book *Start with Why*, I strongly suggest it. In it he introduces readers to the concept of the Golden Circle, as shown on the following page (Sinek n.d.). This Golden Circle informs us why we do what we do as humans. And if we train ourselves to start everything we do by asking, "Why?" it will help us figure out the how and the what. So, before we introduce you to a playbook to help you begin your unboxing journey, it's helpful to start asking more "why" questions, including: "Why should we embark on this change?" "Why will this make a difference for our learners?" "Why will creating a stronger learning culture positively impact our business overall?"

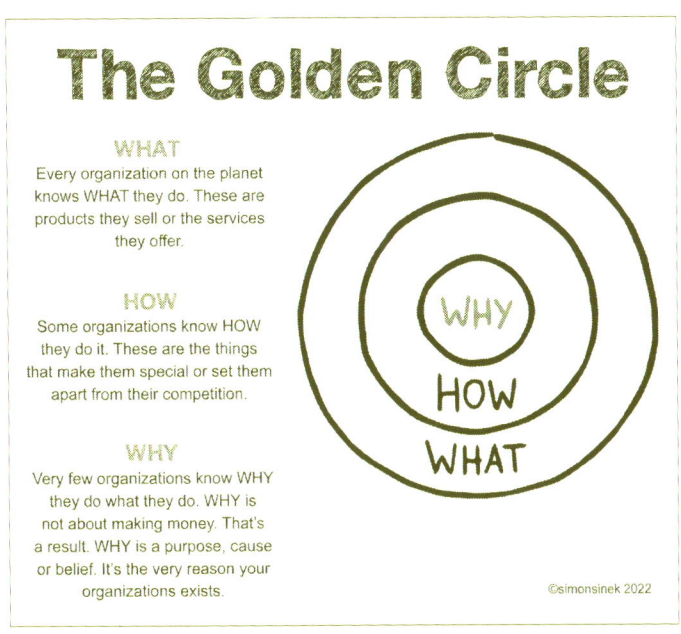

For some reason, this mindset and inquisitiveness is baked into my DNA. I'm always asking "why" questions, like a four-year-old. Why aren't students learning more about technology? Why do teachers still use expensive textbooks? And by the way, why must books be rectangular in shape? Why are we still sitting in classrooms with rows of chairs? Why do we continue doing things that aren't effective or impactful? Why do consumer goods companies keep producing products in packaging that is harmful to the environment (and frankly a waste of money)? Why are people afraid of change? Why are dinner plates round? Why does toilet paper come in a roll? Why, why, why? What's interesting is that the answer to so many of these questions is, "Well, it's always been done this way. Let's just keep doing it that way." That answer is unacceptable.

The subtitle of this book is *Rewiring Your Mindset About Learning*. Notice it doesn't say *Changing the Way You Work*. Yes, I'm driving for that, too, but behavioral changes start with changes in how we think, how we perceive the world around us, and what we value. It is now time to begin a monumental shift from your current mindset about learning to a new one that is wide open to any and all possibilities.

UNBOXING WITH A QUANTUM MINDSET

We have all been living by a code. Throughout this book, we've referred to this code as "the box." Sometimes we're aware of it, but most of the time it operates unconsciously—shaped by our education, culture, and society. If we want to achieve breakthroughs in our field and adopt new ways of thinking, we have to learn how to break this code.

At its core, this code is a program—a foundation upon which our ideas, belief systems, and thought processes are built. When we invite you to "unbox," it's more than a metaphor; it's a call to inspect, evaluate, and, if necessary, crack open your existing code so that you can rebuild it with a new paradigm of thought. In an era where innovation is key to survival, thinking outside the box can no longer be reserved for random brainstorming sessions.

But what if the real problem isn't just the box itself but the way *we think* about it? How do we crack this code?

Quantum physics has revealed that reality is far more fluid than we once believed. At the subatomic level, particles exist in multiple states simultaneously, connections transcend distance, and uncertainty is an inherent part of the system. These principles don't just apply to physics; they apply to the way we think, learn, and innovate.

By applying quantum principles such as entanglement, superposition, the uncertainty principle, and synchronicity, we can break through limitations and redefine the learning experience. Whether you're an educator redesigning your curriculum or a leader driving change in your organization, adopting a quantum lens will allow you to move beyond conventional boundaries into a space of limitless potential.

Now, cracking the code isn't just about breaking free from limitations. It's about rewriting the very rules that shape our reality. When we embrace a quantum mindset, we don't just step outside the box; we dismantle it, reprogramming the underlying structure that governs our thinking. The true breakthrough comes when we stop seeing the code as something to escape and start seeing it as something to reconstruct. In this new paradigm, innovation isn't about pushing boundaries. It's about realizing none existed to begin with.

ADOPTING A QUANTUM MINDSET

Think about the scientific concepts you learned in elementary school—things like gravity, acceleration, and energy. Classical physics teaches us that everything follows clear, predictable rules. If you drop a ball, it falls. If you push something, it moves. Everything has a definitive state. But quantum physics is different. It studies how the tiniest things in nature, i.e., atoms and particles, behave, and it turns out they don't follow the same strict rules. Instead of always being in one state, they can exist in multiple states at the same time until we observe them. This way of thinking is called "first principles thinking" because it breaks things down to their simplest form and builds understanding from there.

Now, what if we applied these concepts to the way we think, make decisions, and solve problems? What if we stopped looking at things as simply right or wrong and started seeing the many possibilities in between? Let's shift from classical thinking to quantum thinking.

We often think in a very black-and-white way. Something is either right or wrong, a success or a failure, possible or impossible. But a quantum thinker, instead of always looking for one "right" answer, learns to embrace the unknown. In the quantum world, things can be in multiple states at once, meaning a single correct solution isn't always available. There can be many.

By thinking this way, we can become better problem solvers, inventors, and leaders—people who aren't stuck in old ways of thinking but are ready to create new solutions for our teams and organizations. As we introduce you to the following quantum concepts, we invite you to think about how you can evolve your thoughts, ideas, and decisions as a learning leader.

Quantum thinking – embracing paradox and possibility: We often search for explicit, definitive answers, but quantum thinking allows us to move beyond absolutes and embrace paradoxes. Remember, in the quantum world, multiple possibilities can exist at once. The same is true for ideas, decisions, and creativity. The key to innovation is learning to hold space for possibilities rather than rushing toward a single, fixed outcome.

Consider the story of Nobel Prize-winning physicist Richard Feynman, who once solved a complex physics problem not by following a standard equation but by approaching it from multiple, seemingly contradictory perspectives at once. By reserving space for different possibilities and resisting the urge to collapse them into a single answer too soon, he unlocked new ways of understanding the problem—an approach that applies just as powerfully to creativity, innovation, and problem solving in any field.

Entanglement – everything is connected: In the quantum realm, particles can become entangled, meaning their states are linked no matter how far apart they are. This isn't just a phenomenon in physics; it's a good representation of how life works. Right? Our thoughts, our behaviors, and our actions don't exist in isolation. Every decision we make influences a larger network of ideas, people, and opportunities. Understanding this helps us approach our careers with greater awareness, knowing that small shifts can create far-reaching impact.

Superposition – holding multiple possibilities at once: As F. Scott Fitzgerald famously says, "The test of a first-rate intelligence is the ability to hold two opposing ideas in mind at the same time and still retain the ability to function." We have already learned that a quantum particle can exist in multiple states at the same time, until it is observed.

Similarly, our greatest ideas emerge when we allow multiple possibilities to coexist instead of forcing a single path or answer too hastily.

Schrödinger's famous thought experiment illustrates this well. Imagine a cat inside a sealed box with a mechanism that could either keep it alive or end its life based on the random decay of an atom. According to quantum mechanics, until we open the box, the cat exists in a superposition—both alive and dead at the same time (Metwalli 2024). Now, apply this to creativity and problem solving. If we insist on certainty too soon, we dismiss possibilities before they've had a chance to evolve. But if we stay open to the unknown, exploring multiple directions at once, we increase our chances of discovering something truly groundbreaking.

Uncertainty principle – growth requires comfort with the unknown: As noted in Werner Heisenberg's book *The Physical Principles of the Quantum Theory*, the uncertainty principle states we can never know both the position and momentum of a particle with absolute precision. The more we focus on one, the blurrier the other becomes (Heisenberg 1949). This isn't just a law of physics; it's a powerful lesson in leadership and life. If we try to control every detail of the future, we limit what's possible. Creativity, growth, and innovation come from exploration, not rigid plans.

Synchronicity – meaningful coincidences lead to breakthroughs: Many of history's greatest discoveries were serendipitous. They weren't planned; they happened when someone was open to unexpected connections. When we shift our mindset to embrace synchronicity, we start noticing patterns, ideas, and insights that guide us toward new possibilities. The key is to stay receptive, allowing unexpected moments to shape our path rather than dismissing them as random or obtrusive.

By moving from a fixed mindset to a fluid one, from rigid thinking to dynamic exploration, we unlock new ways to solve problems. Applying these quantum principles to learning and innovation leads us into a space of limitless potential, where the future isn't just something we predict but something we actively shape.

THE UNBOXING PLAYBOOK

Now that we've explored the mindset and principles behind quantum unboxing, it's time to put these ideas into action. Whether you're a professor, an L&D or HR professional, a K–12 educator, or any other kind of learning leader, keep in mind that the path to growth and success is dynamic, filled with stages of discovery, experimentation, reflection, and expansion.

These seven phases aren't linear. They overlap, loop back, and require you to constantly adapt. The following steps will guide you in applying quantum-inspired thinking to your learning efforts, making unboxing not just a one-time event but an ongoing journey of transformation. We're focusing here on rewiring your mindset. Applying quantum thinking principles should in and of itself blow your mind open. Plus, our minds don't have a maximum capacity like a box does.

> The "paradox" is only a conflict between reality and your feeling of what reality "ought to be."
>
> Richard Feynman,
> American theoretical physicist and Nobel Laureate

Innovation Phase	Phase 1: **Clarity and Vision** Question yourself: Are you clear on your personal core mission or purpose? Does your current role feel aligned with your deeper goals?
Quantum Step	**Define Your Why** *Quantum principle: entangled purpose*
What is it?	Clarify goals using Sinek's Golden Circle. Illuminating the "why" behind your profession is a crucial step. It brings purpose to your actions and aligns your goals with a broader vision. By defining your purpose, you allow yourself to tap into the powerful force of entanglement, where your goals are connected to your larger mission, impacting all your decisions.
Example	The mission behind Edstutia is to revolutionize education by using immersive virtual environments for collaborative learning. Our purpose is entangled with the vision of creating an accessible and engaging educational space where adult learners, regardless of their physical location, can dive into immersive experiences. By leveraging VR, Edstutia allows educators to bring business and soft skills training to life, making learning a deeply interactive experience that transcends traditional classroom boundaries.
Actionable Step	**Action** *Engage in a quantum mapping exercise:* Draw a map that visualizes your current purpose and its potential entanglements—how it connects with people, ideas, and opportunities you haven't yet considered. Reflect on ways your purpose intersects with the broader ecosystem, and refine your mission by asking, "What unseen forces align with my purpose?"

Innovation Phase	Phase 2: **Self-Reflection** Question yourself: What's working well for you? What areas are you struggling with? How would you measure your progress so far?
Quantum Step	**Assess Your Current State** *Quantum principle: quantum measurement*
What is it?	Reflect on what's working in your current role. Reflecting on your current state is essential before moving forward. This step is about taking a quantum measurement of your progress and identifying areas for growth. It's not about placing judgment, but rather creating a snapshot of where you are.
Example	In VR-based medical training, a health care provider may assess their skill set by using VR simulations to test their performance in a controlled environment. VR platforms like Osso VR offer real-time feedback on surgical procedures, allowing trainees to measure their ability before stepping into an actual operating room. This data-driven reflection on the current skill level, akin to quantum measurement, enables practitioners to pinpoint their strengths and weaknesses for continuous improvement.
Actionable Step	**Action** *Conduct a quantum mirror reflection*: Instead of simply evaluating your strengths, use multiple perspectives (from mentors, peers, or even competitors) to understand your true capabilities. Then, engage in a reflective practice where you "collapse your wave function" by identifying the most promising aspect of your growth potential and nurturing that with laser focus.

Innovation Phase	Phase 3: **Exploration and Flexibility** Question yourself: Do you feel you have a clear path in your role but also see multiple potential opportunities? Are you open to new ideas and directions?
Quantum Step	**Plan Your Journey** *Quantum principle: superposition strategy*
What is it?	Set milestones, but stay flexible. This step emphasizes creating flexibility and holding multiple possibilities at once, much like quantum superposition. By setting milestones while staying open to unexpected paths, you leave room for serendipitous breakthroughs.
Example	When Oculus was first developing its VR platform, they didn't just focus on gaming but also considered applications in multiple industries. Initially, Oculus's superposition strategy included branching into health care, training, architecture, and social applications. Their flexible approach to VR technology led to unexpected breakthroughs, such as the use of VR for exposure therapy in treating PTSD. This willingness to explore various possibilities opened up new avenues for innovation, and the platform now serves a multitude of industries well beyond gaming.
Actionable Step	**Action** *Implement a superposition experiment*: List three distinct, "seemingly unrelated" potential paths to a professional goal. Then, work on all three simultaneously for a short period. The goal isn't to follow one path but to discover where the overlap creates unexpected breakthroughs. Reflect on what happens when you don't force a singular path but allow all possibilities to evolve.

Innovation Phase	Phase 4: **Experimentation and Learning** Question yourself: Are you in the process of testing ideas or prototypes? Do you feel comfortable learning through trial and error?
Quantum Step	**Experiment and Iterate** *Quantum principle: uncertainty in action*
What is it?	Test, learn, and adapt. The uncertainty principle teaches us that we cannot predict every outcome with certainty, but we can grow through experimentation. Learning leaders and innovators must be willing to test ideas and iterate, even if they can't predict the outcome at the start.
Example	Magic Leap, a company focused on augmented reality, initially set out to develop a hardware device for fully immersive experiences. However, they soon faced challenges in their first iterations. Instead of sticking rigidly to their original product concept, they embraced uncertainty and iterated their approach, focusing on more practical applications of AR, such as workplace collaboration and design. Through this experimentation, Magic Leap pivoted from a consumer-focused product to enterprise solutions, demonstrating how embracing uncertainty in a rapidly evolving space can lead to greater innovation.
Actionable Step	**Action** *Quantum jumping*: Start a series of micro-experiments where you leap into scenarios of controlled uncertainty. Tackle something small in a completely new way (e.g., testing your assumptions by making a decision without traditional data or advice) to break free from conventional approaches. Track how the unpredictable outcomes lead to insights you couldn't have anticipated through linear thinking.

Innovation Phase	Phase 5: **Collaboration and Networking** Question yourself: Are you seeking help, advice, or partnerships to move your career and objectives forward? Do you have a solid network or need to expand your connections?
Quantum Step	**Build a Support System** *Quantum principle: quantum network*
What is it?	Connect with mentors and peers. Quantum entanglement shows us how everything is connected. Similarly, the support system you build should be a network of influencers who can help propel your work forward. This includes mentors, peers, and collaborators who contribute to your success.
Example	HTC VIVE has built an extensive ecosystem of partners, developers, and collaborators in the VR space, creating a "quantum network" of interconnected individuals and organizations. Their VIVEPORT platform encourages collaboration, allowing developers to showcase their VR experiences and users to explore content from around the world. By fostering this interconnected community, HTC VIVE has enhanced the adoption of its technology and ensured that its VR ecosystem continues to evolve, benefiting from the collective contributions of its global network.
Actionable Step	**Action** *Create a quantum collider:* Instead of just networking with like-minded individuals, seek out those whose perspectives challenge yours. Organize "collision events" (online or in person) where you deliberately mix disparate groups or ideas, fostering dynamic exchanges that catalyze exponential growth and innovation. Engage in conversations that might feel uncomfortable but reveal new perspectives.

Innovation Phase	Phase 6: **Personal Growth** Question yourself: Are you investing time in learning new skills or self-improvement? Are you prioritizing your personal growth?
Quantum Step	**Invest in Yourself** *Quantum principle: energy amplifier*
What is it?	Allocate time and resources specifically for personal growth. Quantum physics teaches us that energy can be amplified when particles interact. Similarly, investing in yourself means dedicating time and energy to your growth, which creates momentum and draws in the right connections, insights, breakthroughs, and resources aligned with your vision. As you build your skills and focus on your goals, you expand your awareness and improve decision-making, allowing success to unfold naturally. Energy flows where focus goes—when you invest in yourself, you create the conditions for the right opportunities to come to you.
Example	Consider the infamous story of Steve Jobs, where he transformed his life and career by deeply investing in his own curiosity and vision. In his early years, Jobs dropped out of college but continued attending classes that genuinely interested him—like calligraphy. This might have seemed insignificant at the time but later influenced Apple's groundbreaking design aesthetics. He immersed himself in the world of technology, collaborating with Steve Wozniak to build the first Apple computer in his parents' garage, attracting investors and like-minded innovators who saw his vision. By dedicating time and energy to his own ideas and skills, he created a magnetic field of innovation—proving that when you invest in yourself, the right opportunities, people, and breakthroughs naturally align to accelerate success.
Actionable Step	**Action** *Quantum energy shifting*: Invest in a "future self" skill—something that seems too advanced or unfamiliar right now. Let go of short-term returns and focus on long-term exponential growth. Try immersing yourself in a field outside your comfort zone, not for immediate results but because your future energy will multiply in unforeseen ways. Track how the new skill opens up unexpected doors or connections.

Innovation Phase	Phase 7: **Expansion and Influence** Question yourself: Have you reached a point where you feel it's time to share your knowledge or influence others? Are you seeing your ideas impact those around you?
Quantum Step	**Scale and Share** *Quantum principle: entanglement effect*
What is it?	Expand your impact. The final step is about scaling your impact and sharing your knowledge. As with quantum entanglement, the more you share your discoveries, the more they influence others, creating a ripple effect across various fields and communities.
Example	The rise of OpenAI and ChatGPT are prime examples of how sharing knowledge and innovation can scale exponentially. OpenAI started as a research initiative focused on advancing artificial intelligence. By making their models accessible to researchers, developers, and businesses, they created an ecosystem where others could build upon and refine their technology. As more people contributed, experimented, and shared their findings, AI applications exploded—leading to breakthroughs in creative writing, coding assistance, education, and countless industries.
Actionable Step	**Action** *Share with a purpose*: Don't just share your insights—create "quantum experiences" for others. Develop a space (digital or physical) where your knowledge is not only shared but also transformed by those who engage with it. For example, run a workshop where participants contribute new insights or ideas to your original concept, amplifying its impact beyond your own reach. Track how this collective wisdom accelerates your influence in new, unpredictable ways.

*More examples and templates provided on our webpage.

SO WHAT? NOW WHAT?

Phew! That was a lot to take in. Does your head feel like it's exploding? Let it all sink in, and take the time to make sense of it. Let's crack the code. Let's unbox. Let's open our minds to allow possibility in. If you've never been exposed to quantum physics terms and quantum thinking concepts, that's okay. I think the components of first principles thinking as presented here are manageable and should be somewhat familiar.

The purpose of this book is to inspire you to walk the walk and be a change agent to reshape the world of learning. The purpose of learning evolves over time; therefore, the learning content and experiences also need to evolve—not as a reaction to change, but to prepare people to embrace and manage said change. Education systems and processes are broken. It is clear we are at a crossroads in time when key stakeholders—students, employees, and employers—are desperate for change.

Thinking outside the box shouldn't be relegated to quarterly brainstorming sessions. It should become the norm for how we live, learn, and operate—and that comes down to being open-minded and agile. So many external forces in our world advance us as human beings, whether we like it or not. What we can't afford to do is ignore what's happening beyond the walls of institutions and organizations. Those buildings might resemble boxes, but our mind is not a box. It is not meant to be suppressed. It is meant to flourish to reach our highest potential.

What lies in store for us if we remove the infrastructure, rules, and policies around formal learning? Total chaos, right? While the change might result in initial chaos for procedures and administrations (maybe, maybe not…), it will certainly result in growth and freedom and opportunity for learners. On the other hand, if we don't adapt, what kind of chaos will result then?

One of my favorite stories I heard while writing this book was from Steve Grubbs, CEO of VictoryXR. To move forward, he says he looks to the past. He mentioned that when he was younger, his father would say, "Those who forget the past are condemned to repeat it." He then shared a story about Sears that was impactful to him. And it left a mark on me as well.

> Everybody knows Sears stores, right?

What most people don't realize is Sears was the first Amazon. They set up shop in Chicago where all the trains were. They sent their catalogs all over America on trains—for free. People would place their orders and send money on the train back to Chicago, and then Sears would ship it out. People bought *houses* this way.

Sears owned the interstate commerce world in the late 1800s and early 1900s due to their train network. Slowly, their entrepreneurs faded away. People who knew they needed to adopt new ways of doing things were gone. And Sears was suddenly run by a bunch of MBAs, not entrepreneurs. And we all know that Sears… Well, it's still around, but barely.

Fast forward…

One guy realizes the same opportunity exists with the internet. He puts a store out on the internet called Amazon selling books. People start ordering books. They place their orders online. Amazon ships out the books from warehouses. It's *exactly* the same model as Sears. And very quickly, he owns the ecommerce world.

What Walmart could have done ten times over... what Sears could have done... they *didn't* do. It took one solo entrepreneur to make a decision to move forward.

So when I try to motivate people, I tell them, "You don't have to be rich. You don't have to have all the advantages. You just have to have the desire to move forward and be able to make the decision to move forward."

Just move forward.

My wish for you is that you see change as something positive and exciting. Be the Uber in a yellow taxicab world. Start by taking one small action today to start your unboxing journey. Referring to your Unboxing Playbook, start by questioning a belief, learning something new, or trying an unfamiliar experience. It doesn't have to be a big lift. It just needs to be intentional. Every step you take toward unboxing creates a ripple effect that can empower you—and others—to break through barriers and redefine the learning experience.

What is important to understand is that unboxing isn't just a concept. It's a movement, a mindset, and a call to action. It's about embracing the unknown, challenging conventions, and continuously reaching beyond what you thought possible. By pairing a quantum mindset with other out-of-the-box ideas mentioned in this book, it will make a drastic difference in your role as a learning leader and in the lives of others. And clearly the impact goes well beyond a classroom or a training room or a virtual space. We have the ability to set our learners up for success for decades to come as the world continues to spin faster.

We'll look back at these ideas for rewiring adult learning ten years from now with a whole new perspective. The students and employees we are mentoring today will in turn be the ones faced with even more ambiguity and unknown problems to solve. Our job as learning leaders is to prepare them for that. And our job as the authors of this book is to continue to provide you with the resources to help you along your own transformational unboxing journey since we know it will also evolve over time.

To that end, you will find a QR code below. We have created a source to keep us connected and share insights. We will also regularly populate the site with updated articles, reports, stories, and more to keep the book relevant versus becoming outdated by 2026. We invite you to join us and visit the site regularly, because this is not the end of a book. This is simply the beginning of living and learning without a box in your way.

Acknowledgments

Yogini and I would like to thank the following people for being a part of our inner author community and coming along for the journey this past year. Your support in the project as well as your belief in us to boldly express our thought leadership with the future of adult learning is genuinely appreciated. Without you, you wouldn't have this book in your hand. Thank you.

Claudine Anderson, Lisa Baldwin, Claire and Paul Blumenfeld, Sabra Brock, Kellie Carroll-Juarez, Caroline Carter, Merry Casperson, Kim Cazani, Matthew Conway, Rob Cordova, Sonali Damle, Rahul Deshmukh, Subodh Deshmukh, Jasmine Devi, Karen and Tom Doran, Tom Duffy, Fred and Joanne Ehrlich, Mike Enos, Larry Epstein, Swaminath Ganesan, Jennifer and Ralph Giordano, Julie Goldman, Patrick Halligan, Sarah and Peter Hammond, Tom Hammond, Tom Harriman, Chason Hecht, Mary Hickey, Erin and Michael Higgins, Bradley Humphries, Irina and Alex Isajeva, Carol and Charles Janssen, Erika and Doug Janssen, Barbara and Eric Johnson, Carla and Paul Johnson, Joanna and Warner Jones, Stephen Kirk, Eric Koester, Jes

Landau, Caryn Lee, Nelia Lokotkova, Amy Lui Abel, Ayesha Madni, Caroline Marquardt, Brent Martini, Kevin McEvoy, Mary McGinty, Tina McNulty, Helga Miedtke, Aditi Mukherjee, Soumya Murthy, Jennifer Neumaier, Abigail Newsome, Sylvain Newton, Philip Nybroten, Barb Ostapina, Kris and Dan Otzelberger, Shelly Parra, Denise and Chris Peterson, Greg Pillar, Lisa Ponti, Vijay Raghavan, Hakan Satiroglu, Leigh Stadler, Deb Stroff, Kiran Suravarapu, Kathy and Rob Taishoff, Carole and Eric Taub, Vrushali Tembe, Marc Torres, Dawn and Jared Vergilis, Elizabeth Walsh, and Jen William.

A huge thanks goes out to all the amazing people who graciously gave up their time to be interviewed for the book:

Matt Alex; Bryan Alexander, PhD; Michael Baston, PhD; Lyron Bentovim; Mark Boccia, EdD; Michael Crow, PhD; Dollie Davis, PhD; Christopher Dede, PhD; Matt Donovan; Tyler Gates; Steve Grubbs; Corey Mohn; Kay Peterson; Brian Rosenberg, PhD; and Nathaly Tschanz.

To our team at Edstutia, we are grateful for all that you contribute to make our vision of "Learning Rewired" come alive. Thank you for your commitment and solidarity.

Ash Balagopal, Sanika Doolani, Jose Gonzalez, Erin Higgins, Stephen Hricko, Xavier LeBlanc, Michele Oberly, Amanda Parks, Renu Ramakrishnan, Anandam Ravi, and Divya Varkey. An extra special thank you goes out to Dr. Sanika Doolani for her contributions in the book, particularly in chapter 11. Her expertise in the worlds of learning and emerging technology made our message that much stronger.

To Yogini, thanks for being such a great writing partner and business partner. I couldn't move this vision forward without you. Forever grateful for your friendship, dedication, and passion.

Massive gratitude goes out to Eric Koester and the Manuscripts team for their amazing support along the way. I wanted to especially thank those who personally coached me this past year: Kristy Carter, Kristy Elam, Carolyn Farias, Angela Ivey, Jill Magnuson, Whitney McGruder, Jacques Moolman, Angela Murray, Gjorgji Pejkovski, and Alexander Pyles. Boy, do you people know how to light a candle under one's rear.

On a personal note, a gigantic thank you goes out to my daughter, Samantha, for being patient with me during this process and for referring to me as her "fly girl." You're mine too. Thank you to my boyfriend and rock, Tom Hammond, for endless support and reassurance as I wrote this book and continue to build out my business. I promise to be a little more present now. I would never be in this fortunate position without the love and support from my mom, Helga, also fondly known as Omi. As a former educator, she saw the need for a book like this to spark some life into the learning experience for people of all ages. And finally, a special shoutout goes to my dear friend Nicole Mene, who is looking down on us from heaven. I love you all.

YOGINI'S PERSONAL ACKNOWLEDGMENTS

This book is dedicated to my gurus in various walks of life who inspire me daily to strive toward lifelong learning and curiosity, humility and accessibility in teaching, and putting "the other" first—whether it is a client, learner, colleague, or family member. I was content to be a writer of journal articles and blog posts until Chris Janssen nudged me out of that box, and I am immensely grateful for her vision and drive in getting *There Is No Box* into your hands. Thank you to our Edstutia colleagues whose professionalism, kindness, and brilliance lights up our days, and to friends and family who have been amazing cheerleaders, sharing their enthusiasm and experiences, supporting our publishing efforts, and cracking "box" jokes along the way to keep it all real.

Appendix

INTRODUCTION

Chan, Roy Y. 2016. "Understanding the Purpose of Higher Education: An Analysis of the Economic and Social Benefits for Completing a College Degree." *JEPPA*. 6, no. 5: 1–41.

No author. 2010. "Did You Know 3.0." vlbworks2010. March 2, 2010. 4:55. https://www.youtube.com/watch?v=jp_oyHY5bug.

CHAPTER 1

Aristotle. 1902. *Nicomachean Ethics*. London: MacMillan & Company, Ltd.

Britannica.com. 2025. *First Universities in the Western Hemisphere*. Chicago: Encyclopedia Britannica.

Brühlmeier, Arthur. 2010. *Head, Heart and Hand: Education in the Spirit of Pestalozzi*. Cambridge: Open Book Publishers.

Damon, William. 2009. *The Path to Purpose: How Young People Find Their Calling in Life*. New York: Free Press.

Dweck, Carol. 2016. "What Having a 'Growth Mindset' Actually Means." *Harvard Business Review*. January 13, 2016. https://hbr.org/2016/01/what-having-a-growth-mindset-actually-means.

Dweck, Carol, and E. L. Leggett. 1988. "A Social-Cognitive Approach to Motivation and Personality." *Psychological Review* 95, 2: 256.

Encyclopedia Britannica. 2025. *Gurukula*. https://www.britannica.com/topic/gurukula.

Gallagher, Sean R., Rashid Mosley, and Tova Sanders. 2021. "The New Landscape for Workplace Learning: Employers and Workers Managing the Digital Transition." *Northeastern University Center for the Future of Higher Education and Talent Strategy*. October 2021. https://cps.northeastern.edu/wp-content/uploads/2021/10/Workplace-Learning-Report-1.pdf.

Ghai, Kavitta. 2022. "Why Are We Still Learning the Same Way We Did 400 Years Ago?" *Edtech Digest*. December 16, 2022. https://www.edtechdigest.com/2022/12/16/why-are-we-still-learning-the-same-way-we-did-400-years-ago/.

Immordino-Yang, Mary H., and Antonio Damasio. 2007. "We Feel, Therefore We Learn: The Relevance of Affective and Social Neuroscience to Education." *Mind, Brain, and Education* 1(1): 3–10.

Maylett, Tracy, and Tim Vandehey. 2023. "'Swiping' isn't Just About Smartphones: The Real Reason Employees Disengage From Training." Training Industry. May 9, 2023. https://trainingindustry.com/articles/performance-management/swiping-isnt-just-about-smartphones-the-real-reason-employees-disengage-from-training/.

Plato. 1955. *Republic*. London: Penguin Books.

The National Advisory Committee on Creative and Cultural Education (NACCCE). 1999. "All Our Futures: Creativity, Culture and Education." May 1999. Report to the Secretary of State for Education and Employment, and the Secretary of State for Culture, Media and Sport. London: DFEE.

WGU.edu. 2022. "Andragogy vs. Pedagogy: Key Differences in Learning." Western Governors University. May 24, 2022. https://www.wgu.edu/blog/andragogy-pedagogy-key-differences-learning2205.html.

Wijesinghe, Gita. 1987. "Indian Philosophy as a Means for Understanding Modern Ashram Schools." *Comparative Education* 23, 2: 237–243. http://www.jstor.org/stable/3098989.

Woo, Elaine. 2019. November 17. "School of Thought." Accessed November 16, 2024. https://rossier.usc.edu/news-insights/news/school-thought.

Workplace Intelligence. 2022. "Study Finds That 74% of Millennial and Gen Z Employees Are Likely to Quit Within the Next Year Due to a Lack of Skills Development Opportunities." October 27, 2022. https://workplaceintelligence.com/upskilling-study/.

CHAPTER 2

Bean, Cammy. 2022. "E-Learning. What Do I Call Thee? Let Me Count the Ways." Kineo.com. January 26, 2022. https://kineo.com/en-us/resources/what-do-we-call-elearning.

Bersin, Josh. 2020. "A New Model for Corporate Training: The Adaptive Learning Organization." JoshBersin.com. November 6, 2020. https://joshbersin.com/2020/11/a-new-model-for-corporate-training-the-adaptive-learning-organization/.

Bligh, Donald A. 2000. *What's the Use of Lectures?* San Francisco: Jossey Bass Publishers.

Bohne, Raphael. 2024. "Market Share of the Market Research Industry Worldwide by Country 2022." Statista.com. November 9, 2024. https://www.statista.com/statistics/491063/largest-share-of-market-research-spending-worldwide/#statisticContainer.

Bright, Jim. 2010. "Chaos theory of careers tutorial: Using the Change Perception Index." *The Factory (blog), BrightandAssociates.com.* September 20, 2010. https://www.brightandassociates.com.au/wordpress/chaos-theory-of-careers-tutorial-using-the-change-perception-index/.

Buck, Daniel. 2023. "In Defense of the Traditional Classroom." Fordham Institute. December 14, 2023. https://fordhaminstitute.org/national/commentary/defense-traditional-classroom.

Bui, Sean. 2022. "What Makes The Completion Rates of Your Online Courses So Low and How to Improve Them?" eLearningIndustry.com. February 13, 2022. https://elearningindustry.com/what-makes-the-completion-rates-of-online-courses-so-low-and-how-improve-it.

Burkins, Lynsey, and Franki Sibberson. 2024. "5 Things Abbott Elementary Gets Right About Public Education." *ASCD* (blog). February 6, 2024. https://ascd.org/blogs/5-things-abbott-elementary-gets-right-about-public-education.

Child, Felipe, Marcus Frank, Jonathan Law, and Jimmy Sarakatsannis. 2023. "What Do Higher Education Students Want From Online Learning?" McKinsey.com. June 7, 2023. https://www.mckinsey.com/industries/public-sector/our-insights/what-do-higher-education-students-want-from-online-learning.

DiPiro, Joseph T. 2009. "Why Do We Still Lecture?" *American Journal of Pharmaceutical Education* 73(8): 137. https://pmc.ncbi.nlm.nih.gov/articles/PMC2828296/.

Faurot, Holly. 2017. "LMS 101: The Evolution of Corporate Learning." Forbes.com. February 7, 2017. https://www.forbes.com/sites/paycom/2017/02/07/learning-management-systems-101-the-evolution-of-corporate-learning/?sh=79109e475e25.

Hattie, John. 2009. *Visible Learning: A Synthesis of Over 800 Meta-Analyses Relating to Achievement.* London: Routledge.

McKeachie, W. J., and Svinicki, M. 2013. *McKeachie's Teaching Tips.* Boston: Cengage Learning.

Muqeet, Bilal. 2021. "4 Levels of Interactivity in eLearning and Its Advantages." eLearningIndustry.com. May 12, 2021. https://elearningindustry.com/levels-of-interactivity-in-elearning-advantages-4.

National Center for Education Statistics. 2022. "US Education in the Time of COVID." Accessed January 20, 2025. https://nces.ed.gov/surveys/annualreports/topical-studies/covid/.

Ong, Joanne, Rebecca De Santo, Jagdeep Heir, Edmund Siu, Nirosa Nirmalan, Martin B. Ofori, Abiola Awotide, Okeida Hassan, Raquel Ramos, Taha Badaoui, Victoria Ogley, Christian Saad, Esteban Sabbatasso, and Susan Morrissey Wyse. 2020. "Seven Missing Pieces: Why Students Prefer In-Person Over Online Classes." *University Affairs.* Accessed January 22, 2025. https://universityaffairs.ca/features/7-missing-pieces-why-students-prefer-in-person-over-online-classes-2/.

Tyton Partners. 2023. "Time for Class of 2023: Bridging Student and Faculty Perspectives on Digital Learning." *TytonPartners.com.* Accessed January 20, 2025. https://tytonpartners.com/time-for-class-2023-bridging-student-and-faculty-perspectives-on-digital-learning/.

CHAPTER 3

Castillo, Evan, and Lyss Welding. 2025. "Tracking College Closures and Mergers." BestColleges.com. January 7, 2025. https://www.bestcolleges.com/research/closed-colleges-list-statistics-major-closures/#fn-1.

Chaturvedi, Anumeha. 2013. "47% Graduates in India are Unemployable For Any Job: Report." *The Economic Times.* June 24, 2013. https://economictimes.indiatimes.com/jobs/47-graduates-in-india-are-unemployable-for-any-job-report/articleshow/20741628.cms?from=mdr.

Dietel, R. J., J. L. Herman, and R. A. Knuth. 2003. "What Does Research Say About Assessment?" https://www.semanticscholar.org/paper/What-Does-Research-Say-About-Assessment-Dietel-Herman/088a2cdbeb2f9e932e5eceda92042ea04390ff76.

Edge Research. 2024. "Student Perceptions of American Higher Education." Gates Foundation. March 11, 2024. https://usprogram.gatesfoundation.org/news-and-insights/articles/student-perceptions-of-american-higher-education.

Fry, Richard, Dana Braga, and Kim Parker. 2024. "Is College Worth It?" May 23, 2024. Pew Research. https://www.pewresearch.org/social-trends/2024/05/23/is-college-worth-it-2/.

Gardner, Michael. 2025. "Survey Shows Growth in International Student Numbers." University World News. January 10, 2025. https://www.universityworldnews.com/post.php?story=20250110113637602.

Gupta, Asha. 2022. "A Case for For-Profit Private Higher Education in India." *Berkeley Center for Studies in Higher Education.* October 2022. https://escholarship.org/uc/item/56d324gm.

Hanson, Melanie. 2025. "Student Loan Debt Statistics." EducationData.org. January 15, 2025. https://educationdata.org/student-loan-debt-statistics.

Intelligent. 2024. "Nearly Half of Companies Plan to Eliminate Bachelor's Degree Requirements in 2024." July 23, 2024. https://www.intelligent.com/nearly-half-of-companies-plan-to-eliminate-bachelors-degree-requirements-in-2024/.

Korn Ferry. 2018. "Future of Work: The Global Talent Crunch." Accessed January 25, 2025. https://www.kornferry.com/content/dam/kornferry/docs/article-migration/FOWTalentCrunchFinal_Spring2018.pdf.

Law, Barbara and Mary Eckes. 2007. *Assessment and ESL: An Alternative Approach.* Winnipeg, Canada: Portage & Main Press.

Maglione, Francesca. 2024. "Half of College Graduates Are Working High School Level Jobs." Bloomberg. February 22, 2024. https://www.bloomberg.com/news/articles/2024-02-22/career-earnings-with-a-college-degree-underemployed-graduates-lag-on-income?srnd=wealth&utm_content=business&utm_source=linkedin&utm_medium=social&utm_campaign=socialflow-organic&cmpid=socialflow-linkedin-business+&leadSource=uverify%20wall.

Mathews, Eldho, and Philip G. Altbach. 2023. "Shortages and Surpluses in HE: The Curious Case of India." University World News. July 1, 2023.
https://www.universityworldnews.com/post.php?story=20230628081508207.

McGurran, Brianna. 2023. "College Tuition Inflation: Compare The Cost of College Over Time." May 9, 2023.
https://www.forbes.com/advisor/student-loans/college-tuition-inflation/.

Mercer | Mettl. 2023. "India's Graduate Skill Index 2023." Accessed January 23, 2025.
https://pages.mettl.com/hubfs/Report%202023/Mercer_Mettl_India%E2%80%99s%20Graduate%20Skill%20Index%202023.pdf.

Mosley, Eric. 2024. "Mind The (Skills) Gap." *Forbes*. May 16, 2024.
https://www.forbes.com/sites/ericmosley/2024/03/26/mind-the-skills-gap/.

National Association of Colleges and Employers (NACE). 2023. "Job Outlook 2023." Spring 2023 Update.
https://www.naceweb.org/store/2022/job-outlook-2023.

National Center for Education Statistics. 2022. "Postbaccalaureate Enrollment. Condition of Education." US Department of Education, Institute of Education Sciences. Accessed January 27, 2025.
https://nces.ed.gov/programs/coe/indicator/chb.

New America. "Student Loan History." Education Policy. Accessed January 25, 2025.
https://www.newamerica.org/education-policy/topics/higher-education-funding-and-financial-aid/federal-student-aid/federal-student-loans/federal-student-loan-history/.

Nink, Marco. 2024. "How Leaders Should Respond to Germany's Stubborn Talent Shortage." Gallup.com. July 26, 2024.
https://www.gallup.com/workplace/647612/leaders-respond-germany-stubborn-talent-shortage.aspx.

Selingo, Jeffrey J. 2025. "Higher Ed's Grim New Normal." *The Chronicle of Higher Education*. January 6, 2025.
https://www.chronicle.com/article/higher-eds-grim-new-normal.

Shauk, Roman. 2025. "Learn Unlearn Relearn: Breaking the Cycle of Failure in Education." EducateMe. January 26, 2025.
https://www.educate-me.co/blog/learn-unlearn-relearn.

UNESCO Institute for Lifelong Learning. 2024. "Sixth Global Report on Adult Learning and Education (GRALE 6): Concept Note." Accessed January 25, 2025.
https://unesdoc.unesco.org/ark:/48223/pf0000391600.

Villeneuve, Marina, and Olivia Sanchez. 2024. "Tracking College Closures." The Hechinger Report. October 21, 2024.
https://hechingerreport.org/tracking-college-closures/.

Woodhouse, Louisa. 2024. "New Report: Cost Remains the Largest Barrier to Higher Ed." National College Attainment Network. September 9, 2024.
https://www.ncan.org/news/681687/New-Report-Cost-Remains-the-Largest-Barrier-to-Higher-Ed.htm.

World Economic Forum. 2025. "Future of Jobs Report." January 2025.
https://reports.weforum.org/docs/WEF_Future_of_Jobs_Report_2025.pdf.

CHAPTER 4

Akçayir, Murat, Hakan Dündar, and Gökçe Akçayir. 2016. "What Makes You a Digital Native? Is It Enough to be Born After 1980?" *Computers in Human Behavior.* 60 (July 2016): 435–440.

Bennett, Sharon. 2019. "The Experience Age Has Arrived." *BA Times.* February 19, 2019. https://www.batimes.com/articles/the-experience-age-has-arrived/#:~:text=The%20%E2%80%9CExperience%20Age%E2%80%9D%20is%20one,becomes%20the%20product%20%E2%80%94%20an%20experience.

Bersin, Josh. 2018. "A New Paradigm For Corporate Training: Learning in the Flow of Work." JoshBersin.com. July 8, 2018. https://joshbersin.com/2018/06/a-new-paradigm-for-corporate-training-learning-in-the-flow-of-work/.

Blitz, Matt. 2017. "The History of the All You Can Eat Buffet." *Food & Wine.* June 22, 2017. https://www.foodandwine.com/news/enlightenment-age-swedes-vegas-gamblers-history-all-you-can-eat-buffet.

Buglione, Suzanne and Felice Billups. 2023. "Adult Learners: Now What?" The Evolllution. July 23, 2023. https://evolllution.com/revenue-streams/market_opportunities/adult-learners-now-what#:~:text=Adult%20learners%20want%20learning%20environments,and%20applicable%20to%20their%20lives.

Drucker, Peter. 1996. *Landmarks of Tomorrow.* New York: Routledge.

ELM Learning. 2022. "8 Characteristics of Adult Learners Every L&D Pro Should Know." ELM Learning. February 11, 2022. https://elmlearning.com/blog/who-are-adult-learners/.

Hanover Research. 2024. "Engaging and Recruiting Gen Z Students in Higher Education." *Higher Education Insights, Hanover Research.* March 15, 2024. https://www.hanoverresearch.com/insights-blog/higher-education/engaging-and-recruiting-gen-z-students-in-higher-education/.

Linkletter, Karen. 2024. "The Future of Knowledge Work." Management as a Liberal Art Institute. September 16, 2024. https://mlari.ciam.edu/the-future-of-knowledge-work.

Oppland, Mike. 2016. "8 Traits of Flow According to Mihaly Csikszentmihaly." PositivePsychology.com. December 16, 2016. https://positivepsychology.com/mihaly-csikszentmihalyi-father-of-flow.

Pappas, Christopher. 2023. "The Adult Learning Theory—Andragogy—of Malcolm Knowles." eLearning Industry. September 8, 2023. https://elearningindustry.com/the-adult-learning-theory-andragogy-of-malcolm-knowles.

Radjou, Navi, Jaideep Prabhu, and Simone Ahuja. 2011. "Use Jugaad to Innovate Faster, Cheaper, Better." Harvard Business Review. December 8, 2011. https://hbr.org/2011/12/think-like-an-indian-entrepren.

Saleem, Lakshmi. 2018. "The Refined Self: Healed-up Souls." YouTube TED Talk. January 2018. 16:49. https://www.ted.com/talks/dr_lakshmi_saleem_the_refined_self_healed_up_souls?subtitle=en.

Teo, Lynette. 2023. "Reaching the 'Digital Natives:' Effective Training Delivery for Gen Z." Training Industry. August 8, 2023. https://trainingindustry.com/articles/strategy-alignment-and-planning/reaching-the-digital-natives-effective-training-delivery-for-gen-z/#:~:text=Training%20should%20be%20personalized%2C%20technology,over%20traditional%20lecture%2Dstyle%20training.

Thompson, Julie. 2023. "From Texting to Tweeting: Tech-Savvy Millennials Are Changing the Way We Work." *Business*. May 10, 2023. https://www.business.com/articles/tech-savvy-millennials-at-work/.

Wang, Jia. 2024. "Understanding a Multigenerational Workforce." Metals Service Center Institute. January 16, 2024. https://www.msci.org/understanding-a-multigenerational-workforce/#:~:text=By%202025%2C%20millennials%20will%20account,they%20are%20engaged%20at%20work.

Wiley, Sandra. 2020. "Understanding Today's Generational Differences in the Workforce and Technological Preferences." FirmoftheFuture.com. February 6, 2020. https://www.firmofthefuture.com/running-a-business/understanding-todays-workforce-generational-differences-and-the-technologies-they-use/.

World Economic Forum. 2024. "The Intelligent Age: A Time for Cooperation." September 24, 2024. WorldEconomicForum.org. https://www.weforum.org/stories/2024/09/the-intelligent-age-a-time-of-cooperation/.

CHAPTER 5

Acorn. 2024. "Your Guide to the L&D Metrics That Matter for Proving the ROI of Learning." https://acorn.works/blog/learning-and-development-metrics#what-are-learning-and-development-metrics-.

Acorn. 2025. "Non-Negotiable LMS Reporting and Analytics Tools." https://acorn.works/resource/lms-reporting-and-analytics.

Betterworks 2024 US Research Report. 2024. "Skill Fitness: Powering the Skills-Based Organization with Performance Data." https://skillsreport.betterworks.com/.

Cappelli, Peter, and Anna Tavis. 2016. "The Performance Management Revolution." Harvard Business Review. October 2016. https://hbr.org/2016/10/the-performance-management-revolution.

Caron, Betsy. 2011. "UpToDate System Saves Lives, Time and Improves Quality Care." Healthcare Finance News. November 23, 2011. https://www.healthcarefinancenews.com/news/uptodate-system-saves-lives-time-and-improves-quality-care

Drexler, Madeline. 2020. "Bridging the Know-Do Gap." Harvard T.H. Chan School of Public Health. May 29, 2020. https://hsph.harvard.edu/health-policy-management/news/bridging-the-know-do-gap/.

Duncan, Tisha, and Allison A. Buskirk-Cohen. 2011. "Exploring Learner-Centered Assessment: A Cross-Disciplinary Approach." *International Journal of Teaching and Learning in Higher Education* 23, 2: 246-259.

Gupta, Disha. 2022. "11 Innovative Ways to Measure Training Effectiveness." Whatfix Blog. October 17, 2022. https://whatfix.com/blog/measure-training-effectiveness/.

Kazmi, Asyia. 2024. "Can AI Transform Education?" Gates Foundation. September 11, 2024. https://www.gatesfoundation.org/ideas/articles/ai-tools-education-technology.

Kruk, Margaret, E. and Muhammad Pate. 2020. "The Lancet Global Health Commission on High Quality Health Systems 1 Year On: Progress on a Global Imperative." *The Lancet—Global Health.* January 2020. https://www.thelancet.com/journals/langlo/article/PIIS2214-109X(19)30485-1/fulltext

Verlinden, Neelie. n.d. "The Talent Management System in a Nutshell." Academy to Innovate HR. n.d. https://www.aihr.com/blog/talent-management-system/.

Webber, Ashleigh. 2019. "BridgeCon Europe: The Role of L&D in Creating 'Purposeful' Work." Personnel Today. November 25, 2019. https://www.personneltoday.com/hr/learning-and-development-purposeful-work/.

xAPI. n.d. "xAPI Solved and Explained." https://xapi.com/?utm_source=google&utm_medium=natural_search.

CHAPTER 6

Center for Creative Leadership. 2022. "The 70-20-10 Rules for Leadership Development." CCL.org. April 24, 2022. https://www.ccl.org/articles/leading-effectively-articles/70-20-10-rule/.

Davidson, Cathay N. and Christina Katopodis. 2022. "10 Arguments for Inciting Learning." Inside Higher Ed. July 19, 2022. https://www.insidehighered.com/advice/2022/07/20/why-active-learning-more-effective-traditional-modes-opinion.

Deslauriers, Louis, Logan S. McCarty, Kelly Miller, Kristina Callaghan, and Greg Kestin. 2019. "Measuring Actual Learning versus Feeling of Learning in Response to Being Actively Engaged in the Classroom." Proceedings of the National Academy of Sciences, 116 (39).

Emelo, Randy. 2013. "Four Easy Tactics to Engage Your Passive Learners." Association for Talent Development. June 14, 2013. https://www.td.org/content/atd-blog/four-easy-tactics-to-engage-your-passive-learners.

Freeman, Scott, Sarah L. Eddy, Miles McDonough, Michelle K. Smith, Nnadozie Okoroafor, Hannah Jordt, and Mary Pat Wenderoth. 2014. "Active Learning Increases Student Performance in Science, Engineering, and Mathematics." *Proceedings of the National Academy of Sciences.* 11, no. 23: 8410–8415.

Peterson, Kay and David A. Kolb. 2017. *How You Learn is How You Live: Using Nine Ways of Learning to Transform Your Life*. San Francisco: Berrett-Koehler Publishers.

Pink, Daniel H. 2011. *Drive: The Surprising Truth About What Motivates Us.* New York: Riverhead Books.

The Yale Ledger. 2023. "The Best Ways to Learn a Language According to Research." *The Yale Ledger*. December 19, 2023. https://campuspress.yale.edu/ledger/the-best-ways-to-learn-a-language-according-to-research/.

Zull, James E. 2002. *The Art of Changing the Brain.* 1st edition (October 1, 2002) New York: Routledge.

CHAPTER 7

Bersin, Josh. 2010. "High-Impact Learning Culture: A New Era in Corporate Learning & Development." Bersin & Associates. September 2010. https://joshbersin.com/wp-content/uploads/2016/11/2010_LEARNING_CULTURE.pdf.

Bradley, Neil. 2022. "What Is a Learning Culture? Part 1 of 4." TrainingIndustry.com. February 22, 2022. https://trainingindustry.com/articles/strategy-alignment-and-planning/what-is-a-learning-culture-part-one-of-four/#:~:text=This%20definition%20is%20 %E2%80%9Ca%20culture,and%20goals%20of%20the%20organization.%E2%80%9D.

Deloitte Insights. 2019. "Leading the Social Enterprise: Reinvent with a Human Focus." 2019 Deloitte Global Human Capital Trends. https://www2.deloitte.com/content/dam/insights/us/articles/5136_HC-Trends-2019/DI_HC-Trends-2019.pdf.

Fennell, Andrew. 2024. "Top 5 Skills You Need to Get Hired in 2024." FastCompany.com. January 21, 2024. https://www.fastcompany.com/91014141/top-5-skills-you-need-to-get-hired-in-2024.

Lundberg, Abbie, and George Westerman. 2020. "The Transformer CLO." Harvard Business Review. January-February 2020. https://hbr.org/2020/01/the-transformer-clo.

Marr, Bernard. 2023. "The 10 Most In-Demand Skills in 2024." Forbes.com. November 27, 2023. https://www.forbes.com/sites/bernardmarr/2023/11/27/the-10-most-in-demand-skills-in-2024/?sh=1c99c0b57397.

Mosley, Eric. 2024. "Mind The (Skills) Gap." *Forbes*. May 16, 2024. https://www.forbes.com/sites/ericmosley/2024/03/26/mind-the-skills-gap/.

World Economic Forum. 2023. "Future of Jobs 2023: These Are the Most In-Demand Skills Now—and Beyond." WorldEconomicForum.org. May 1, 2023. https://www.weforum.org/stories/2023/05/future-of-jobs-2023-skills/.

CHAPTER 8

Accenture. 2021. "Meeting the New Reality: Immersive Learning." Accenture Insights. September 14, 2021. https://www.accenture.com/us-en/insights/technology/immersive-learning.

Alam, Faisal and Matt Barrington. 2023. "Is The Future of Your Tech Stack Built on the Foundation of Your People?" Ernst & Young Insights. June 12, 2023. https://www.ey.com/en_us/insights/consulting/how-talent-feels-about-emerging-tech?WT.mc_id=10852271&AA.tsrc=paidsearch&gad_source=1&gclid=CjoKCQjw6uWyBhD1ARIsAIMcADpE4MQgghKnjQE028C73J5-PzHkyNEltZvdjjAbpeisCOAwkBg1coaAjRFEALw_wcB.

Baraishuk, Dmitry. 2023. "Adaptive Learning AI Technology in Education." Belitsoft. July 13, 2023.
https://belitsoft.com/custom-elearning-development/ai-in-education/adaptive-learning-ai.

Cairns, Rebecca. 2023. "Could the 'Metaversity' be the College Campus of the Future?" CNN World. June 27, 2023.
https://www.cnn.com/2023/06/28/americas/metaversity-virtual-reality-morehouse-college-hnk-spc-intl/index.html.

Duolingo Team. 2023. "Introducing Duolingo Max, a Learning Experience Powered by GPT-4." Duolingo. March 14, 2023.
https://blog.duolingo.com/duolingo-max/.

Educause. 2024. "2024 Educause Horizon Report: Teaching and Learning Edition." Educause. May 13, 2024.
https://library.educause.edu/resources/2024/5/2024-educause-horizon-report-teaching-and-learning-edition?gad_source=1&gclid=CjoKCQjw6uWyBhD1ARIsAIMcADoUJBrF7KLB0YEb6k7C-alhM18nB_4Tkmk_3ENckQSEBzv4XMlAVWIaAr6PEALw_wcB.

Fink, Charlie. 2021. "This Week in XR: The Quest Turns Two, Accenture Buys 60,000 for Training." Forbes. October 21, 2021.
https://www.forbes.com/sites/charliefink/2021/10/21/this-week-in-xr-the-quest-turns-two-accenture-buys-60000-for-training/.

HRD Connect. 2023. "VR Onboarding: How Accenture Is Redefining HR with Metaverse Technology." HRD Connect Case Studies. February 13, 2023.
https://www.hrdconnect.com/casestudy/how-accentures-enterprise-metaverse-has-elevated-employee-onboarding/.

Kanaki, Marialena. 2025. "From Data to Action: Predicting and Enhancing Learner Success." eLearning Industry. February 18, 2025.
https://elearningindustry.com/from-data-to-action-predicting-and-enhancing-learner-success#:~:text=Predictive%20analytics%20is%20a%20game,diverse%20needs%20of%20every%20employee.

LinkedIn. 2024. "Workplace Learning Report 2024." Accessed September 5, 2024.
https://learning.linkedin.com/content/dam/me/business/en-us/amp/learning-solutions/images/wlr-2024/LinkedIn-Workplace-Learning-Report-2024.pdf.

Markets and Markets. 2024. "Extended Reality Market Size, Share and Trends." Markets and Markets. Report Code: SE 7890. December 2024.
https://www.marketsandmarkets.com/Market-Reports/extended-reality-market-147143592.html.

Marr, Bernard. 2023. "A Short History of ChatGPT: How We Got to Where We Are Today." Forbes.com. May 19, 2023.
https://www.forbes.com/sites/bernardmarr/2023/05/19/a-short-history-of-chatgpt-how-we-got-to-where-we-are-today/

MDA Training. 2024. "The 11 Game-Changing L&D Trends of 2024." LinkedIn. January 15, 2024. https://www.linkedin.com/pulse/11-game-changing-ld-trends-2024-mda-training-az5nf/.

Meier, Ellen, Caron Mineo, Kraken Kirsch Page, and Seth McCall. 2023. "Transforming Education or Digitizing the Status Quo?" Association for Supervision and Curriculum Development. June 26, 2023. https://ascd.org/el/articles/transforming-education-or-digitizing-the-status-quo.

Mordor Intelligence. 2024. "Virtual Reality (VR) Market Size, Share, Growth Trends, Industry Statistics & Consumer Analysis (2025–2030)." Mordor Intelligence. 2024. https://www.mordorintelligence.com/industry-reports/virtual-reality-market#:~:text=The%20Virtual%20Reality%20Market%20size,to%20create%20an%20artificial%20environment.

Pratt, Mary K. 2023. "Explore 14 Real-world Use Cases for Adaptive AI." TargetTech.com. October 2, 2023. https://www.techtarget.com/searchenterpriseai/tip/Explore-real-world-use-cases-for-adaptive-AI#:~:text=Adaptive%20AI%2C%20however%2C%20would%20enable,will%20meet%20the%20customer's%20needs.

Terehin, Andrew. 2023. "How to Enhance Your LMS with Big Data & Learning Analytics." Agente Studio. August 15, 2023. https://agentestudio.com/blog/lms-big-data.

WEKA. 2022. "What Are Big Data & Predictive Analytics? How Do They Relate?" WEKA. November 17, 2022. https://www.weka.io/learn/ai-ml/big-data-predictive-analytics/#:~:text=Big%20data%20refers%20to%20the,patterns%20to%20forecast%20future%20events.

CHAPTER 9

Art of Play. 2016. "History of the Nine Dot Problem." Art of Play. August 2, 2016. https://www.artofplay.com/blogs/stories/history-of-the-nine-dot-problem#:~:text=The%20first%20known%20publication%20was,dots%20likely%20predate%20Loyd's%20eggs.

Brown, Brené. 2011. "The Power of Vulnerability." TED. January 3, 2011. 20:49. https://www.youtube.com/watch?v=iCvmsMzlF70.

Dweck, Carol S. 2006. *Mindset: The New Psychology of Success*. New York: Penguin Random House LLC.

Hill, Tamara. 2018. "Atychiphobia: 3 Signs You Fear Failure." PsychCentral. December 5, 2018. https://psychcentral.com/blog/caregivers/2018/12/atychiphobia-3-signs-you-fear-failure#1.

Klein, Gary. 2023. "Shifting Mindsets: What Does It Take?" *Psychology Today*. March 20, 2023. https://www.psychologytoday.com/us/blog/seeing-what-others-dont/202303/shifting-mindsets-what-does-it-take.

Pink, Daniel H. 2022. *The Power of Regret: How Looking Backward Moves Us Forward*. New York: Riverhead Books.

Sackstein, Starr. 2019. "What Does It Mean to Be in Control in Education?" *EducationWeek.* July 19, 2019. https://www.edweek.org/teaching-learning/opinion-what-does-it-mean-to-be-in-control-in-education/2019/07.

CHAPTER 10

Woodward, Matthew. 2025. "Zoom User Statistics: How Many People Use Zoom in 2025?" Search Logistics. February 20, 2025. https://www.searchlogistics.com/learn/statistics/zoom-user-statistics/.

CHAPTER 11

Heisenberg, Werner. 1949. *The Physical Principles of the Quantum Theory.* Garden City, NY: Dover Publications.

Metwalli, Sara A. 2024. "What Is Schrödinger's Cat?" Built In. March 7, 2024. https://builtin.com/software-engineering-perspectives/schrodingers-cat#:~:text=Schr%C3%B6dinger's%20Cat%20is%20a%20thought,(or%20may%20not)%20occur.

Robbins, Tony. n.d. "How To Create Positive Energy." Accessed August 2, 2024. https://www.tonyrobbins.com/mental-health/creating-positive-energy/.

Sinek, Simon. n.d. "The Golden Circle." Simon Sinek's Optimism Company. Accessed August 2, 2024. https://simonsinek.com/golden-circle/.